T0208658

Upon This Rock

*Building a Firm Foundation
that Cannot Be Shaken*

ROSIE RIVERA

WESTBOW°
PRESS
A DIVISION OF THOMAS NELSON
& ZONDERVAN

WestBow Press books may be ordered through booksellers or by contacting:

WestBow Press
A Division of Thomas Nelson & Zondervan
1663 Liberty Drive
Bloomington, IN 47403
www.westbowpress.com
1 (866) 928-1240

ISBN: 978-1-4908-4942-3 (sc)
ISBN: 978-1-4908-4941-6 (e)

Library of Congress Control Number: 2014915093

Printed in the United States of America.

WestBow Press rev. date: 9/26/2014

Contents

Acknowledgments

All praise and glory be to my Lord and Savior, Jesus Christ, who has given me the knowledge and wisdom I have today through the study of His Word. I can truly say that without Him I am nothing, without Him I have nothing, and without Him I can do nothing. He definitely is my rock and my salvation, in whom I put my trust, and the light and love of my life.

I want to thank my husband, Robert, for his patience during the writing of this book and his encouragement along the way. When I'd grow weary, he'd keep me focused and he never failed in strength. He is the other love of my life.

I also acknowledge the ministers who helped me grow in the Word; they may never know how much I appreciate them and how much help they were to me, but God knows their labor of love; may He reward them greatly.

Personal Experience

Upon This Rock is inspired by my own personal experience in my quest for knowing the almighty God of the universe.

My journey began in 1979 in a small country church. I have no idea what the message was about. I only remember finding myself responding to the invitation at the end of the service. I can still hear the invitation song being sung: "Softly and tenderly Jesus is calling, calling, O sinner, come home." How could I refuse such an invitation? I was looking for some place to belong. Although that song carried me to the altar, it couldn't carry me much further. I soon found myself needing something more but didn't know exactly what it was or how to obtain it.

My search for God was on. I had experienced a love and tenderness I hadn't known before, but after a few weeks, I wondered where that feeling went. I felt alone and abandoned by my newfound love. Surely He must be a God who hides Himself.

Is this where many Christians find themselves after accepting Jesus into their lives? Is this the reason so many Christians fall by the wayside? The questions began: What do I do now? Where do I go from here? Where can I find the answers to my questions? I have a Bible, but I don't understand it. Who can help me understand what I'm reading?

I had been given a Bible, so I thought, If I want to know God, I should be able to find Him in the Bible, right? Wrong. It brought confusion, discouragement, and disappointment. I couldn't understand any of it. It all seemed foreign to me. I knew about God and Jesus, but that's about as far as it went. I didn't know that being a Christian meant a change in lifestyle and an ongoing process of renewing my mind. I asked, where and how does this change begin? Am I going to change automatically or is something going to be required of me? What do I have to do to be pleasing to God?

When you embark on a journey to a destination where you've never been before, the trip is much easier when you have a tour guide. It's much easier to have one who leads the way, one who has gone before you, one who has blazed a trail through the difficulties and challenges you will surely encounter on your journey. I learned some things in church, but it didn't fill the emptiness I felt in my heart. I didn't know where to turn or whom to ask for help. One day while clicking through the channels on TV, I came across a preacher teaching the Word. As I listened, I became more and more interested in what he was saying. I had never heard that kind of preaching. It was through hearing this teacher and others talk about this wonderful Savior of ours that my desire to know Him became my quest in life.

I like the way the apostle Paul said it. Paul had such a desire to know God that it became his determined purpose.

> [For my determined purpose is] that I may know Him [that I may progressively become more intimately acquainted with Him, perceiving and recognizing and understanding the wonders of His Person more strongly and more clearly], and that I may in that same way come to know the power overflowing from His resurrection [which it exerts over believers], and that I may so share His sufferings as to be continually transformed [in spirit into His likeness even] to His death, [in the hope]. (Philippians 3:10 AB)

My quest for God took me down many uncharted paths. One day I would be on the mountaintop rejoicing in my newfound revelation of God and His Word, and the next I would find myself in the valley facing challenges I had never faced before, wondering where God was now that I needed Him.

As I wandered through the valley of uncertainty feeling alone, I noticed that I was beginning to grow in knowledge, understanding, and patience. I found that fruit grows in the valley, not on the mountaintop. One does not have to seek for God when He can clearly be seen. It's during those times when God seems to hide Himself and seems so far away that we begin to seek Him more, and as we seek Him in prayer and the Word, we begin to grow in knowledge and understanding.

I experienced those silent years when God is silent, and I wanted so much to hear Him speak to me, to lead me, to let me know He hadn't left me, that I was not alone. That's when I learned to walk by faith and to trust God even though I couldn't feel His presence. He promised in His Word never to leave me or forsake me.

Tests and trials are a part of life; they cannot be avoided. If we could learn early on in our walk with God that tests and trials come only to make us grow stronger, we wouldn't be so quick to stumble and fall every time we find ourselves under pressure. We can use the tests and trials of life as stepping-stones that can take us to the next level or they can become stumbling blocks that hinder our growth and our walk with God. It's a choice we have to make. It took me a while to learn to take the tests and trials I encountered and use them to my advantage. I learned to use them to help me grow in wisdom and understanding. Tests and trials can be compared to detours that take a person off the path of righteousness; as we veer off the path it becomes harder to get back on track. We have an enemy who is always trying to cause failure in our lives and will always take advantage of us when we are weak. He will tell us how rotten we are, how we failed God, and how God is disappointed with us, and make us feel unworthy of God's love. That is why it is so important to read the Word and know our enemy and how he operates so that we can recognize the strategies and lies of the Devil.

Every journey must have a destination. Today we have GPS systems to guide us to our destinations. They give direction and instructions along the way. The Bible is the Christian's GPS system.

The Word of God is our tour guide that is going to guide us as we begin and finish our journey. We are moving on to maturity in Christ and a great experience in the knowledge of Him. Are you ready to embark on this journey? Buckle up your seat belts and let's go!

Upon This Rock

When Jesus came into the region of Caesarea Philippi, He asked His disciples, saying, "Who do men say that I the Son of Man am?" So they said, "Some say that thou art John the Baptist: some, some Elijah, and others Jeremiah, or one of the prophets." He said to them, "But who do you say that I am?" Simon Peter answered and said, "You art the Christ, the Son of the living God." Jesus answered and said to him, "Blessed art thou, Simon Bar-Jona: for flesh and blood has not revealed this to you, but My Father who is in heaven. "And I also say to you that you are Peter, and on this rock I will build My Church; and the gates of Hades shall not prevail against it. (Matthew 16:13–18 NKJV)

Introduction

This book is intended as a study aid for individuals and group studies, an aid in establishing new believers in the Word of God so they can build a firm foundation that cannot be shaken.

What does it take for new believers to grow and flourish in the Word? For new believers to be able to grow and flourish as Christians, they must be rooted and grounded in the Word of God and in their love for the Lord.

What we do once we are born again depends on how much understanding we have of the price Jesus paid for our redemption. I believe that if one has an understanding of the suffering that Jesus went through to purchase our redemption, it motivates one to become a productive member of the body of Christ. Motivation is what produces a desire to get involved and help others. Church is all about people, and one's main focus should be on helping people become all that they can be for the Lord, and helping them find God's plan for their life, go after it, and fulfill it. Our love for the Lord is what motivates us to love people as He did.

My concern is that many new believers are falling by the wayside because of the revolving door that exists in our churches. It is well known that people come into the church, get born again, and get excited about God. Some even cry, and the conversion seems genuine. We might see them for a few services, but then we don't see them anymore. Why does this happen? I questioned the Lord about it. Where does the solution to this dilemma lie? What is it going to take to keep our new converts from going back into the world? What are our new converts being taught?

We as ministers have a great responsibility to the Lord to see that every new believer has an opportunity to become rooted and grounded in the Word of God, that every new believer has the same opportunity to become a disciple of the Lord and a productive member of the body of Christ.

The foundation is the most important part of a building. That is what determines the amount of pressure the building is going to be able to withstand. As Christians, our foundation is what determines if we are going to be able to stand against the tests and trials of life or if we are going to fall by the wayside. If one's foundation is weak, one's structure will also be weak, and when the tests and trials of life appear, that person is going to be standing on shaky ground. Many Christians start out well but quickly run out of steam, and when tests and trials come their way, they quickly stumble and fall. Many Christians fall by the wayside and never recover.

God never promised us that we were going to float through life on clouds of ease. He never promised our problems would disappear when we became Christians. In all actuality, your problems will most likely increase, but be of good cheer: you are going to learn how to handle them better. You are going to encounter many obstacles as you grow, but you are going to be able to overcome them instead of being overcome by them

> Whoever comes to me, and hears my sayings and does them, I will show you whom he is like: "He is like a man building a house, who dug deep and laid the foundation on the rock, and when the flood arose, the stream beat vehemently against the house, and could not shake it, for it was founded on the rock. But he who heard and did nothing is like a man who built a house on

the earth without a foundation, against which the stream beat vehemently; and immediately it fell. And the ruin of that house was great." (Luke 6:47–49 NKJV)

Jesus says three very important things here; He says "whoever comes to me, and hears my sayings and does them, I will show you whom he is like." There's more to coming to the Lord than just getting born again. One must go a step further and hear what the Word says and do it. Jesus said the foolish man builds his house upon the sand, and when the wind and rain beat upon it, that house cannot remain standing but quickly falls. The wise man builds a firm foundation upon the rock so that when the storms come, they won't be able to knock the house down. We want to build our lives upon the rock of God's Word.

Notice that the same storms come to the house built upon the rock as to the house built upon the sand. What makes the difference is the kind of foundation each house was built upon. The storms of life are going to come to saint and sinner alike. It's going to depend on the foundation one builds whether one is going to stand or fall when the tests and trials of life come.

It reminds me of the children's story "The Three Little Pigs." The first two built their houses out of weak materials, and when the wolf came he huffed and puffed and blew their houses down. They didn't want to take the time to build a stronger house—no, they wanted it done quickly so they could have more time to play. While the other two played, the third little pig was busy building his house out of sturdy material that would stand whenever the wolf came huffing and puffing trying to knock it down. Many Christians find themselves too busy with other things and don't take time to build a foundation that is strong, so when the troubles come, they don't know what to do.

Christianity is not a bed of roses. As soon as you make a decision to follow the Lord, you are going to encounter opposition from every angle. Jesus said when one hears the Word, Satan comes immediately to take away the seed that was sown in their heart. He has to do it immediately because it would be detrimental to him to give the seed time to grow and become rooted in their heart. It's easy to go outside with a small shovel and dig up a newly planted tree. It's much more difficult to uproot a tree that has been standing for several years and has put down roots and is firmly established. Just as a tree needs nourishment and care to grow, so do we Christians need the nourishment of the Word of God to grow and become productive Christians.

I strongly stress the importance of studying and getting acquainted with the Word of God. If you study the Word and get it down in your spirit, that Word will begin to take root in your heart and begin to establish you so that you cannot be moved, no matter what comes. It is important to read the Word of God as often as you can, to meditate on it, and to put it to work in your daily life. It's the practice of the Word that is going to make you strong and establish you as one who cannot be moved by adverse circumstances.

I thank God for the ministers who taught me the importance of learning the Bible and helped me establish my life on a firm foundation. I was born again in a little country denominational church where I learned about salvation and rededication, but I wasn't taught the Word of God.

I was hungry to know about God so immediately after being born again, I began to study the Bible. But I found there were many things I didn't understand, and there was no one available to teach me. I began to listen to radio and television ministers, and as I listened and learned, a firm foundation of the Word of God was being established in my life.

Over and over I heard, "Make the Word of God priority in your life." What does that mean? It means that when tests and trials come my way, the first thing I ask myself is what does the

Bible have to say about this situation? Thirty-three years have come and gone since the day I got born again, and I am still practicing putting the Word in first place, and it has paid off wonderfully. I have never gone back into the old ways, nor have I been tempted to. I owe it all to those faithful men and women who cared enough about others to teach them how to apply the Word of God to their lives. I have had my share of tests and trials like everyone else, but I've been able to keep on standing because my foundation is built upon the rock of God's Word.

I have dedicated my life to teaching the Bible. My desire is for every human being to get born again and begin to grow up in the Word of God and become established so that when the storms of life come, they will not find themselves lost and without direction but will stand firm, fully persuaded that they can overcome.

When one's foundation is strong, the storms may come and the winds may blow, but that foundation cannot be shaken because it is established upon the rock of God's Word and faith in it. The Word of God must come off the pages of the Bible and become rooted in one's heart.

(Romans 10:17 NKJV) So then faith comes by hearing and hearing by the Word of God.

In order for faith to come, there must be teaching of the Word. Faith doesn't come from having heard; it comes by hearing and hearing and hearing until it gets down in your spirit and becomes a part of you. You may be one of those who say, "I've already heard that." Maybe you have, but what are you doing with what you've heard? Hearing is the easy part; the doing is the hard part. Doing takes effort.

The Bible says there are carnal Christians and there are spiritual Christians, because many Christians think all there is to becoming a strong Christian is attending church on Sunday and Wednesday. A carnal Christian is one who is flesh ruled; he allows his carnal desires to rule his actions. The spiritual

Christian on the other hand is spirit ruled; his actions are controlled by the Word. He is a doer of the Word and not a hearer only.

If you are a hearer and not a doer, you are deceiving your own self. Deception comes when you believe you don't have to hear anymore because you've heard it preached before. Just because one hears preaching, it doesn't mean that one is capable of living a victorious life. Preaching doesn't change a man or woman, but the application of the revealed Word does. When we become doers of what is revealed to us and begin to put the Word to work in our daily lives, the Word becomes real to us because of the results we are seeing. How are we going to know it works if we are not practicing what it says?

This book can be used as an aid or personal study in helping new believers grow in the Word and build their lives on a firm foundation. My prayer has always been "Lord, teach me to divide correctly the Word of truth." I do not want to deceive anyone. I want to help people grow in God's Word so that they can become productive Christians. The Lord placed in the church prophets, evangelists, pastors, and teachers to mature the saints to prepare them for the work of the ministry.

> And He Himself gave some to be apostles, some prophets, some evangelists, and some pastors and teachers, for the equipping of the saints for the work of the ministry, for the edifying of the body of Christ, till we all come to the unity of the faith and of the knowledge of the Son of God, to the perfect man, to the measure of the stature of the fullness of Christ: that we should no longer be children, tossed to and fro and carried about with every wind of doctrine, by the trickery of men, in the cunning craftiness of deceitful plotting, but speaking the truth in love, may grow up in all

things into Him who is the head—Christ—from whom the whole body joined and knit together by what every joint supplies, according to the effective working by which every part does its share, causes growth of the body for the edifying of itself in love. (Ephesians 4:11–16 NKJV)

God placed the fivefold ministry in the church to equip the believer for the work of the ministry. We are all called to work in the ministry in one way or another. Not all are called to a pulpit ministry, but each member of the body of Christ has something to offer—something that helps the body grow stronger. We are joints in the body that join one part to another. God wants us to be fitly joined together so that there are no weak links in the body. We've all heard it said that a chain is only as strong as its weakest link. And so it is with the body of Christ (the church). The stronger we are in the Word, the stronger the link.

God doesn't want His children tossed to and fro with every wind of doctrine and the cunning craftiness of men whose only desire is to deceive people. There are many deceivers out there who are waiting for weak Christians to miss it, to fail, to miss the mark so they can come in with condemnation and deception. Wolves always prey on the weak. We are currently living in the last of the last days, and there are many deceivers waiting for those who are weakest. If there is no firm foundation, it makes it easy for people to be tossed to and fro with every wind of doctrine because they don't know what the Bible says, thus making it easy to stray from the truth and become deceived by the doctrines of men.

I want to help people become established in the Word of God because that is the only means of preventing deception. That is what is going to make people strong in the Lord so that they will know the truth and be able to stand against the wiles of the Devil and be able to know the difference between the doctrine taught by the Word of God and the doctrines taught by men.

Then Jesus said to those Jews who believed Him, "if you abide in my word, you are my disciples indeed. And you shall know the truth and the truth shall make you free." (John 8:31-32 NKJV)

It is vitally important that all new believers study the Word of God. Many come into the kingdom of God bound by traditions of religion and traditions they grew up with that are contrary to the Word of God. Traditions are hard to break. Jesus said "your traditions make the Word of God of none effect," so traditions are powerful—powerful enough to cause the Word of God not to work.

The Word of God teaches us who we are in Christ; it teaches us what Jesus accomplished through His life, His death, His burial, and His resurrection and ascension, so that we can let go of the past that has held us in captivity and take hold of the life God has prepared for us.

I believe the more we understand the Bible, the more we are capable of understanding why we must be born again, what happens when we receive Jesus as our Lord and Savior, and why it is necessary for us to become rooted in the Word and become productive members of the body of Christ.

God has a plan for every born-again believer. The only way to find out what that plan is, is to study the Word of God, find out what the Word says about God's plan and His will, and then apply it to one's life.

What a mighty army of believers we would have on this earth if every believer was equipped to do the work of the ministry and every believer was firmly established in the Word of God, with a foundation that could not be shaken. What changes would take place in this world with such a mighty army! Just think of the tragedy it would be for a soldier to go to war without training, without weapons, and without knowledge of the enemy. Then think what a difference it makes when a soldier is well equipped, knows his weapons, and knows his enemy, and is ready to fight every battle that comes his way. That soldier goes into battle with a winning attitude instead of one of defeat.

The church is in a spiritual battle, and we as good soldiers must go through boot camp to become well-disciplined and prepared. The Word of God is what it takes to prepare you for the battles of life, the battle that goes on daily inside of you between your spirit and your flesh, the thoughts that constantly run through your mind, and the battles that come against you from without.

You can be well prepared for whatever comes your way, ready to stand your ground and ready to overcome every battle. It takes a working knowledge of the Word of God along with discipline and self-control and other things we'll learn as we study the Word of God.

Before one can be recognized as a soldier in the army of God, one must enlist in God's army by being born again.

Chapter 1

Why Must I Be Born Again?

"Jesus answered and said to him, 'Most assuredly, I say to you, unless one is born again, he cannot see the kingdom of God'" (John 3:3 NKJV).

A man named Nicodemus who was a ruler of the Jews had come to Jesus by night. Why he came by night we aren't told; possibly as a ruler he didn't want to be seen by his followers. He knew Jesus was come from God because he was doing things no other man had done. When he spoke to Jesus, Jesus responded by saying that unless one was born again, one could not see the kingdom of God. Nicodemus was puzzled because he didn't understand how a grown man could enter into his mother's womb once again and be born. Just the thought seemed like an utter impossibility. Then Jesus said to him, "Most assuredly, I say to you, unless one is born of water and of the Spirit, he cannot enter the kingdom of God. That which is born of the flesh is flesh; and that which is born of the Spirit is spirit'" (John 3:5–6 NKJV).

Nicodemus was still puzzled. He could not understand how this could be, so Jesus went on speaking to him In John 3:16-17 NKJV, "For God so loved the world that He gave his only begotten Son, that whoever believes in Him should not perish but have everlasting life, for God did not send His Son into the world to condemn the world, but that the world through Him might be saved.

Maybe you're as puzzled as Nicodemus was. Perhaps you're asking, how may I be born again? What do I have to do?

Jesus said, "You must be born again." The word must is a strong word. It means "to be forced to, to have to, and to be obligated to do something." It indicates a requirement or an absolute. The requirement here is that one be born again before seeing the kingdom of God or entering the kingdom of God. It means that for one to be born again, something is required of that person. A person can't just come into the kingdom of God uninvited.

You wouldn't try to go into the White House uninvited, would you? Neither can you enter into God's kingdom uninvited. God extends an invitation to you through the open arms of Jesus and His death upon the cross.

God requires a new birth because of Adam and Eve's sin. Sin left a gap between God and man, and the only thing that can bridge that gap is being born again. To understand why this is an absolute, one must go back to the beginning and find out what actually took place when humanity fell and how as a consequence all people became separated from God.

When one is born into this world, one is born with the sin nature that separates people from God. This nature causes a person to lack the ability to perceive the things of God.

It all goes back to the garden of Eden when God made humanity in His image (Genesis 2:26) and placed the first man and woman in the garden, giving them one commandment: that of the tree in the midst of the garden, the tree of Knowledge of Good and Evil, they should not eat, because in the day they ate of it, they would surely die. God placed in that garden everything the first couple needed to sustain life. God gave them dominion over the earth.

Adam was created before any other creature According to the second account of creation in Genesis 2:18. Then God decided it was not good for the man to be alone, so out of the ground,

He formed every beast of the field and every bird of the air, and brought them to Adam to see what he would call them. Adam named all the cattle and all the birds, but for Adam there was not found a suitable helper. The Lord God caused a deep sleep to fall on Adam, and as he slept, God took one of his ribs and made a woman, according to Genesis 2:21–22. Some jokingly say that's the reason men don't understand women.

We don't know how long it was before the Serpent (the Devil) came into the garden and began to put thoughts into Eve's mind about the tree in the midst of the garden. It could have been months or years, but one thing we know for sure is that he came in subtly. He began by putting thoughts in her mind; that's one way he deceives people. He told Eve that she would not die if she ate of the fruit, but that she would be like God, knowing good and evil. She began to think about what he said. Those thoughts began to work on Eve's mind. She began to think God hadn't told them everything, that there was something lacking, something God was keeping from them.

Isn't that the way the enemy works? People are always searching for that one thing that is going to bring them fulfillment. When God created the first man and woman, He created them in His image, male and female. He created them and gave them dominion over everything except the tree in the midst of the garden.

I imagine Eve began to look at the tree differently. It looked innocent enough. It didn't look like it could kill anyone, and it appeared to be good for food, something worthy of her desire. As she continued looking at the tree, it became more and more appealing, until one day she just couldn't resist the temptation anymore. She took of the fruit and ate, and then gave some to her husband, who was there with her. No, he wasn't out somewhere tending the garden; the Bible tells us he was there with her.

They did not die that day, not physically, but they did become separated from the life of God. Since that day every human being born into this world is born with a void that only God can fill. That's the reason people seek fulfillment in things like riches, fame and fortune, drugs and sex, and other things that never offer lasting satisfaction. That's the reason Jesus came to set the captives free. Sin held us captive. We could never escape from this bondage on our own without a mediator, someone to stand in the gap for us, someone who was innocent without spot or blemish, one who could take our place and pay the penalty for our sin.

Our Lord Jesus Christ came to give us that new life, that missing link that would once again reunite us with the Father. He is the only one who can fill the void in our spirit. When we repent of our sins and receive Him as our Lord and Savior, we become what the Bible calls born again.

"For God so loved the world that he gave His only begotten Son, that whoever believes in Him should not perish but have everlasting life" (John 3:16 NKJV).

God sent His Son to die for us so that we could have eternal life. We couldn't save ourselves. We were slaves to sin. No matter how hard we tried, we couldn't change ourselves. We lived with the constant frustration of trying to do better, just to find ourselves right back where we started. Each of us owed a debt that we could never pay. Romans 6:23 says that the wages of sin is death. We were born into this world with the sin nature, separated from the spiritual life of God. But when we are born again, our spirits receive a brand new birth and we now have the nature of God in our spirits.

Each person is a three-part being. He or she is a spirit, has a soul, and lives in a body. We contact the spiritual realm with our human spirits, the physical world with our bodies and the five physical senses, and the world of the intellect with our souls. The human soul contains the mind, the will, and the emotions.

When you were born again, your spirit was born again. Your soul and your body still need to be trained to submit to the Word of God. Nothing happened to your soul and body when you were born again, so the soul has to be renewed with the Word of God. The body has to be brought into subjection, because it will follow whichever one is in charge, whether it is your spirit or your soul.

The Devil is the enemy of your soul, but he's not as much of an enemy as your flesh is. The flesh is the soulish part of you, and the mind-set of the flesh is against the Word of God.

When you begin to renew your mind with the Word of God, your flesh will rebel, because the flesh wants to rule. It has been in control all this time. Galatians 5:17 says that the flesh lusts against the spirit. The flesh doesn't want what the spirit has. The spirit of God now lives in you, and your new identity is now in Christ. The flesh still wants you to identify with the flesh, or the old nature. The flesh wants you to identify with your intellect, with your physical characteristics, and with your abilities.

The flesh wants you to do things in your own way, with your own ability, instead of depending upon God. The Bible says, "Trust in the Lord with all your heart, and lean not on your own understanding; in all your ways acknowledge Him, and He shall direct your path" (Proverbs 3:5 NKJV).

It is not wise to lean on your own understanding, because your understanding will change with circumstances. When you lean on the Lord, He is reliable, He never changes, and He is the one on whom you can depend. So when you are established in God's Word, you can lean on it, because leaning on that Word is the same as leaning on the Lord.

Because of the weakness of the flesh, people still commit sin after they are born again. The only difference now is that born-again people do not practice sin. Before people were born again, sin was a lifestyle for them. Sin does not have to rule your life any longer, because now you have the grace of God to help you overcome sin. You have to stop trusting in yourself and your abilities and begin to trust God, to lean on Him. It's liberating to know that as a born-again believer, you are no longer enslaved to sin.

God began a work in you the day you were born again, and He is working in you every day, but you have to cooperate with Him.

Sin always has consequences. Sin is progressive. The result of sin is not manifested immediately when one sins. It may begin as a thought, and then evolve into something imagined. Then there's the actual committing of the act. If one does not learn how to control one's thoughts, those thoughts will one day become an imagination, and then as one meditates on the imagination, it takes control of that person's mind.

The sin nature gave Satan the right to dominate mankind. When sin entered the world, sickness, disease, and death came with it. The enemy held that death threat over man's head until Jesus came and set man free from the fear of death. The Devil knows that man's number one fear is the fear of dying. Mankind needed a Savior, one who was both God and man, one who could relate to mankind yet was without sin. Jesus took upon Himself the form of a man so that He could bridge the gap between God and mankind. Jesus became that perfect mediator between God and mankind.

People were programmed to think according to their reasoning, to act and talk according to the ways of the world with no conviction of any wrongdoing. Our spirit was separated from the life of God so that we had no consciousness of sin. "Everybody's doing it," the saying was; if it feels good, do it—with no knowledge of the consequences.

But be doers of the Word and not hearers only, deceiving yourselves (James 1:22 NKJV).

God's Word is our instruction manual on how to live a life that is pleasing to Him. The Word of God was given to us to teach us His will for our lives. If we go to church but never put the Word of God into practice in our lives, we deceive ourselves into thinking we are pleasing God by going to church. Many people think going to church is what pleases God rather than a lifestyle change, which shows God we are learning and applying the Word to our lives daily. The church was instituted to help the believer grow in the Word of God and to help him become a doer of the Word, thus producing fruit that glorifies God.

It's not how much we know that is pleasing to God but what we do with what we know. God doesn't want us to have a head full of knowledge. He wants to see change in us. The more we understand the Word of God and the more we put it to work in our lives, the stronger we become. When our foundation is established on God's Word, we are able to withstand more, and that understanding will cause us to come out victorious in the tests and trials of life. If we always put God and His Word first in our life, we can have the assurance that we will lead a victorious life, and we will succeed at whatever we set our hand to.

God gave us His Word so that we can build our lives on a firm foundation that is unmovable and cannot be shaken. There are not too many things in our world today that we can say are built upon a firm foundation. Everything is shaky: our economy is unstable, the housing market is unstable, and the future is unstable. Only the Word of God can give us the assurance we need to advance in an unpredictable world.

In Scripture we find out what true doctrine is, we find reproof and correction to keep us on track, and we find instruction in righteousness to keep us going in the right direction.

You may be thinking, how can I know the Bible is the Word of God? We know the Bible is the Word of God because of the evidence of a changed life through being a doer of the Word.

"All Scripture is given by inspiration of God, and is profitable for doctrine, for reproof, for correction, for instruction in righteousness, that the man of God may be complete, thoroughly equipped for every good work" (2 Timothy 3:16–17 NKJV).

7

The Amplified Bible says "Every Scripture is God-breathed (given by inspiration0 and is profitable for instruction, for reproof and conviction of sin, for correction of error and discipline in obedience, [and] for training in righteousness (in holy living, in conformity to God's will in thought, purpose, and action), So that the man of God may be complete and proficient well fitted and thoroughly equipped for every good work."

God wants His people to be thoroughly equipped. He wants a people whose desire is to find His will for their lives, and to become productive Christians in the midst of this crooked generation.

When people are born again, they become new creations in Christ, just as if they never existed before. They receive a new nature created in the image of God. This takes place in one's spirit, but one still has the mind and the flesh to deal with.

"Therefore, if anyone is in Christ, he is a new creation; old things have passed away; behold, all things have become new" (2 Corinthians 5:17 NKJV).

If you can grasp this one truth—that you are now a new creation in Christ and that your past has passed away, and that all things are made new—you will have far fewer problems with the way you think. Your past failures, mistakes, and regrets can't keep you from going forward; neither can they hinder you from becoming what God created you to be. The enemy of your soul doesn't want you to get hold of this truth because he knows it will set you free and keep you free.

When people are born again, their spirits receive new life, but they still have minds that must be renewed by the Word of God and bodies that must be brought under subjection to the spirit. The change is not going to come overnight. It takes time, just as in the natural world it takes time to grow up and mature. A baby doesn't come into this world fully grown, with the ability to think and reason at birth. He has to be bathed, changed, fed, clothed, and taken care of. He grows by progression until he is able to take care of himself. So it is with Christians. There is a growth progression that each one has to go through before he becomes a mature Christian.

Many Christians' growth is being hindered by issues of the past. Whatever was done in the past is exactly that: it's in the past. You cannot change it. No amount of guilt or regret can change the things that were done in the past. There's nothing you can do about it except believe that old things have passed away and all things have become new in Christ. You cannot dwell on the past, because it's difficult to move forward while looking back. The enemy of your soul would love to have you live in the past, to have you live your entire life with thoughts of guilt and regret.

The Bible says that God has thrown your sins into the depths of the sea. As far as the east is from the west, that's how far He has removed them from you, but that's not all: He has promised that He will remember your sins no more. It's not God who reminds you of your sins, it's the enemy who wants to keep you bound to the past because he knows that if he can keep you looking back, you can't move forward.

Chapter 1 Questions

1. What does God require for one to be born again?
2. What caused separation between God and man?
3. What is man searching for?
4. Is there something or someone who can fill that void?
5. Man is a spirit; he has a _____, and he lives in a body.
6. Which part of man receives the new birth?
7. What does the Bible require mankind to do with his soul and body?
8. Man is a three-part _____.
9. When one is born again, one becomes a new _____ _____.
10. Man cannot _____ himself.

Chapter 1 suggested reading

Matthew 4:17 … John 3:3
Genesis 3
2 Thessalonians 5:23
Romans 12:1–2
2 Corinthians 5:17

Chapter 1 Answers

1. The requirement for one to be born again is for one to acknowledge one's sin and receive Jesus Christ as one's Lord and Savior.
2. The separation between God and mankind was caused by sin, man's disobedience to God.
3. Man is searching for someone or something to fill the void in his heart.
4. Jesus Christ is the only one who can fill that void.
5. Man is a spirit; he has a soul, and he lives in a body.
6. The spirit of man receives the new birth.
7. Man has to renew his soul and body with the Word of God.
8. Man is a three-part being.
9. When one gets born again, one becomes a new creature.
10. Man cannot save himself.

Chapter 2

Growing Up Spiritually

"'Go therefore and make disciples of all the nations, baptizing them in the name of the Father and of the Son and of the Holy Spirit, "teaching them to observe all things that I have commanded you; and lo, I am with you always, even to the end of the age.' Amen" (Matthew 28:19–20 NKJV).

There are three things we should take note of in this Scripture passage: number one, make disciples; number two, baptize them; and number three, teach them to observe all that I have commanded you. A disciple is one who follows, in this case one who follows the commandments of the Lord.

Teaching is a very important aspect of making disciples. A disciple cannot follow what he does not know; therefore, making the Word of God plain and easily understood must be the priority of any teacher of the Word.

Just as one has to grow up physically, one must also grow up spiritually. Just as growing up physically takes time so does growing up spiritually. First of all, it takes the right nourishment for the body and the right nourishment for the spirit. For the body we understand it takes food to nourish it and make it strong. For the soul we need intellectual nourishment that comes from learning and gaining knowledge about life, and for the spirit we need spiritual nourishment that comes from the Word of God. It takes years of learning, discipline, dedication, and desire to become all that one can be for the Lord.

12

There are many Christians who never grow up and who never lead productive lives because they are unable to leave the past behind. They are living a life of shame and regret over a past they cannot change. This is one of the reasons I'm writing this book. God wants us to grow up and live the abundant life that Jesus has provided for us. The enemy knows that if one can get hold of the truth of God's Word and one will dare to believe, the Devil can't keep that person down. He can't keep that one defeated, he can't intimidate him, and he can't lord it over him, because that person has become an overcomer.

The Bible tells us that we were dead in our sins and trespasses, walking according to the course of this world, according to the prince of the power of the air, the spirit who now works in the sons of disobedience" (Ephesians 2:2 NKJV)

It's easy to go with the flow. It doesn't take any effort to follow the crowd, to do what everyone else is doing; just follow the current wherever it takes you. Once a person has become a Christian that person must change the direction in which he or she was going and began to flow upstream, so to speak, going against the flow. Those who don't know the Lord are going in the opposite direction of what the Word teaches.

We conducted ourselves in the lusts of the flesh, fulfilling the desires of the flesh and the mind and were by nature children of wrath but God, because of his great love for us and his great mercy, even when we didn't deserve it, He made us alive together with Christ and raised us up together with Him and made us sit together in heavenly places in Christ Jesus. (Ephesians 2:5-6) When Jesus was raised from the dead, you were raised together with Him. God now sees you seated together with Christ, no longer dead in your sins and trespasses but alive in Christ! That is the way God wants you to see yourself, as a new creature in Christ, seated with Him. Isn't it wonderful to have joint seating with Christ?

Now that I'm born again, what do I have to do to grow up in Christ and be profitable to the kingdom of God?

Throughout this book I will refer to growing up in Christ as a lifestyle change. Without changing your lifestyle, you will continue to be dominated by the sin nature. God has taken care of the sin nature, but the desires of the old nature are still embedded in you until you make some changes in the way you speak, act, and respond according to the Word of God. The more you study the Word of God, the more it becomes a part of you so that when adverse situations arise, you respond according to the Word and not according to your old nature. The old nature wants to get even, it wants revenge, and it wants to say things it shouldn't say. As you grow in knowledge of the Word, you begin to gain wisdom and understanding about how to conduct yourself in any given situation.

To grow up in Christ one must first understand what the characteristics of the old nature are: how the unregenerate mind thinks, how the flesh responds to circumstances, and how one has conducted one's life without Christ.

We were bound by sin. Sin was our master, a hard taskmaster; we were separated from the life of God. We couldn't change what we were doing because of the sin nature that was in us. It didn't take any effort to sin; it just came naturally to us. Everyone else was doing it; we were unable to see anything wrong with sin because we had no consciousness of wrongdoing. Our eyes were blinded by the selfish desires of the flesh. We were ruled by the five physical senses. We followed the course of this world not knowing that it was leading to destruction. According to the Word of God, there are two ways, and one must choose the right way.

"Enter by the narrow gate; for wide is the gate and broad is the way that leads to destruction, and there are many who go in by it. Because narrow is the gate and difficult is the way which leads to life, and there are few who find it" (Matthew 7:13–14 NKJV).

Many people are going the way that leads to destruction and don't even know it because sin has blinded their minds. Jesus Christ shows us the way that leads to life. The road that leads to life is difficult because it is narrow and compacted. It's not an easy way, but it's the best way. Yes, it's difficult in the beginning, but as one grows in the things of God, one begins to experience victory over circumstances. As one grows, the road gets easier to travel.

Those who don't know the Lord, and even some who know Him, are traveling the wide road because to the natural mind that would seem like the road of choice. It's wide and broad; many are traveling on it, so the reasoning is that it must be good. What they don't realize is that the easy way is not always the best way. Many Christians choose to travel the wide road because they haven't grown up spiritually and it seems to present less opposition, fewer problems, and less responsibility. God Himself told us which road to choose. He said, "Choose life that you and your descendants may live" (Deuteronomy 30:19). God gives us the right to choose our destinies.

God created man with the ability to choose, and He will never violate that right. He will tell a person what is right, what to choose, and which way to go, but ultimately it's up to the individual to make the right choice. The choices you make affect not only you but those closest to you. Adam and Eve made the wrong choice by eating from the tree that the Lord told them not to eat of. They didn't realize the effect it was going to have upon them—not only upon them but ultimately all mankind.

God sent His only begotten Son, Jesus, to die for all humanity and make a way for man to be free from the effects of sin, but He didn't take away man's ability to choose. God doesn't want us to follow Him because we are forced to do it; He wants us to choose to follow Him because we love Him and we believe it is the right way.

Jesus said, "I am the way, the truth and the life, no man comes to the Father but by me" (John 14:6 NKJV).

Jesus' death on the cross provided a better way for us. This is what the Bible calls the narrow road or the new and living way because it leads to eternal life.

Adam's sin affected not only our spirit it also affected our soul and our body. We became subject to sickness, disease, and death. We began to reason with our mind and became soul ruled.

Mankind became the product of sin and death. We were separated from God, we had no inheritance or hope, and we were limited in our approach to God. Man was in need of a mediator, one who could stand in the gap, one who could take hold of God with one hand and man with the other, one who was acquainted with our weaknesses and our sorrows, one who could approach God without sin. Jesus was that mediator sent from God in the form of man so that He'd be able to relate to us. The Bible tells us that He was tempted in all points as we are, yet without sin, which is why He is able to understand what mankind goes through. He overcame sin in the flesh and conquered death and did it all for us so that we could be reconciled to the Father.

When you were born again, God became your heavenly Father, freeing you from the sin nature. That doesn't mean you are perfect. We're moving toward perfection. We are still governed by the five senses and ruled by circumstances, still self-seeking and following the course of this world until our mind is renewed by the Word of God. It's not the outer man where change took place; the change took place in our spirit, so we have to work with our spirit and train the mind and the body to obey the Word of God.

Christian growth is progressive. You aren't born again one day and then automatically know how to live the Christian life. You have to start out as a baby in Christ, and as you study the

Bible, you begin to grow spiritually. First Peter 2:2 says that as newborn babes we should desire the pure milk of the Word, that we may grow thereby.

The Word of God is spiritual food for one's spirit. Just as one needs nourishment for one's body to grow, one needs spiritual nourishment to grow spiritually.

When we begin to grow in the Word of God, we learn to be governed by what God says. Circumstances become stepping-stones for building our faith. We're no longer self-seeking but seek the good of others. Our mind is being renewed by the Word of God. We learn how to apply the Word to our circumstances to cause them to change; we become doers of the Word and not hearers only.

God has a plan for your life that only you can fulfill. The Bible says that God began a good work in you and that He will develop it, perfect it, and bring it to completion. He is not going to leave that work undone. He will keep working with you until you have reached perfection or maturity.

The Amplified Bible says, "For we are God's (own) handiwork (His workmanship) recreated in Christ Jesus, (born anew) that we may do those good works which God predestined (planned beforehand) for us (taking paths which he prepared ahead of time), that we should walk in them (living the good life which he pre-arranged and made ready for us to live)" (Ephesians 2:10).

You are God's own handiwork! You have been recreated in Christ Jesus so that you can do the good works that God prepared ahead of time for you to do. He has prepared paths for you to walk in so that you can live the good life that Jesus came to provide for you.

The Bible is your guidebook. It is your manual for life. The Word is what you want your foundation to be built upon. When your foundation is built upon the Word of God, you become established in the truth, which will make you an overcomer in life.

As far as God is concerned, you are beginning a brand new life. As you grow, you will begin to see many changes take place. Your thinking will change, your desires will change, and your way of talking will change, and you will begin to see a change in the way you respond and react to people and circumstances.

Your nature has changed from darkness to light. You have gone from death unto life. Your dead spirit is now alive unto God. If you understand that you are a three-part being—you are a spirit, you have a soul, and you live in a body—then you can understand that although your spirit received instant transformation, you still have to do something about your soul and your body. The Bible calls it the flesh.

The soul contains the mind, the will, and the emotions. You have to bring your soul into subjection to the Word of God. Man was once spirit ruled, but after the fall he became soul ruled. By that, I mean man began to reason and to question God's authority. Now you must renew your mind to think the way God thinks, surrender your will to your spirit, and bring your emotions in line with the Word of God. The soul is the place where decisions are made, and those decisions influence the way we think, the way we perceive things, and the way we feel. If we don't change the way we think, or renew our minds, our decisions will be based on what we perceive through the five physical senses and will be unstable and unpredictable.

Unless you renew your mind with the Word of God, your soul is being ruled by your emotions, and emotions are not a safe guide. Emotions change with circumstances. Selfishness is the nature of the soul. It has a "me" mentality. The unregenerate mind thinks on the things that gratify the flesh. The flesh is going to follow the soul or the spirit, depending on which is strongest. The Bible says that if we walk in the spirit, we will not fulfill the lusts of the flesh (Galatians 5:16).

According to the Bible, the lust of the flesh, the lust of the eyes, and the pride of life are of this world, and they are the things that bring one down. (1 John 2:16) These are the things the world seeks after because they are the things that gratify the desires of the flesh. A person who has not been born again walks according to the desires of the flesh as was mentioned in an earlier chapter.

It takes time and patience to develop into the kind of person who is able to control the desires of the flesh and bridle the tongue. The tongue, as the Bible says, is a very small member in the body, but it can set things on fire, it can put others down, or it can lift them up; it can bless or it can curse. The Bible says the tongue is full of deadly poison, but the man who is able to control the tongue is a wise man, a mature man. Proverbs 18:21 tells us that death and life are in the power of the tongue and that we eat the fruit of it, whether it be of life or of death (my paraphrase).

It's very important that we learn to speak words of life rather than words of death. We pick up phrases here and there that sound good, but they have no life in them. For example, I'm dying to go, or It's killing me, or I'm a wreck, or Everything I do is a failure. What we don't realize is that words carry power. Words are containers. They are carriers of life or carriers of death. To speak negatively is to speak death; to speak positively is to speak life. We have been programmed by the ways of the world to see things negatively and then speak accordingly. The Bible teaches us to speak positively so that our words produce good results.

"Whoever guards his mouth and tongue, keeps his soul from troubles" (Proverbs 21:23).

A person who watches what he or she says keeps his or her soul from troubles. Most of mankind's problems begin with words. There's a saying that goes like this: sticks and stones may break my bones, but words will never hurt me. According to the Word of God, that is not true. The Bible tells us that words wound, words cause contention, and words destroy.

Most of humanity's problems are caused by people's inability to control their tongue. That is why the Bible has so much to say about the words of one's mouth. Words affect how you see yourself and how others see you. If you have a positive attitude, people will notice, and if you have a negative attitude, they will notice also.

Proverbs 18:14 tells us that it is easier to sustain a physical infirmity than it is to sustain a wounded spirit.

We all know people who have been wounded in their spirits. It takes some people years to recover from a wounded spirit, and others never do. If you have small children, I encourage you to speak positive words to them because the words we speak to a child can affect the way that child sees himself. Positive words produce a positive attitude and a positive outlook on life. I encourage you to be careful how you say things, especially when you're upset. Words can cause separation between good friends and destroy good relationships.

It is important that when we are born again, we begin to see ourselves as God sees us. God has a different perspective of you than the world has. God sees you dead unto sin and alive unto God. He sees you free from the law of sin and death, free from condemnation. He sees you as more than a conqueror, and victorious. No one has arrived; every one of us is on our way to perfection. God is doing a work in you, progressively bringing you to completion.

"And I am convinced and sure of this very thing, that He who began a good work in you will continue until the day of Jesus Christ (right up to the time of His return), developing (that good work) and perfecting and bringing it to full completion" (Philippians 1:6 AB).

God is going to continue working on you right up to the time of His return. He is going to perfect that work and bring it to full completion as long as you continue in His Word and continue to put it into practice in your life. There are no perfect human beings. We are all at different stages of perfection. It's Him doing the work in you. It begins with hearing the Word, yielding one's self to Him and putting what one learns to work in one's life. Next year you will be a year closer to perfection. You will continue to grow because God's Word can never be exhausted, no matter how many times it is read. You will continue to receive new revelation according to what you are able to handle. You will learn how to rightly divide the the word of truth.

God has predestined you for change. You are predestined to be conformed into the image of Christ. God will use every opportunity to see to it that you continue to grow. Every test, every trial, and every temptation that comes your way is an opportunity for growth. One day you will be able to see how these things either hinder or help your growth. Life is made up of the choices you make. You are going to find that your life has been patterned after choices and decisions that you have made in the past. What determines whether those choices are going to make you or break you is the attitude you have toward the situations you face. Attitude is how you respond mentally or emotionally to the circumstances of life.

The Word of God gives instruction about how we are to conduct ourselves by putting away the former conversation or our former conduct, or the way we formally responded to tests and trials of life, by putting away lying and anger and not allowing corrupt communication to come out of our mouths.

John the Baptist called Jesus the Lamb of God. John was a forerunner of Jesus. He was sent to prepare Israel to meet their Messiah. The first time John saw Jesus, he exclaimed, "Behold the Lamb of God who takes away the sin of the world." The Pharisees and Sadducees were upset because they didn't think they needed to change; they lived according to the law. John came preaching repentance and baptizing those who repented and believed in their need for change. He required them to bring evidence of a repentant life. God requires us to bring evidence of

Rosie Rivera

a repentant life. That evidence is in how we conduct ourselves, the change in our character, and the way we talk.

Jesus is God come in the flesh. Isaiah, one of the prophets, called him Emanuel, meaning "God with us." He is the express image of God. He is the one whom man could see and touch, the one man was able to relate to. People were afraid of God. The Old Testament tells us that God had come down on a mountain once to visit the children of Israel. There was lightning and thunder and the mountain quaked so that the people feared and asked Moses to hear for them what God had to say to Israel. After that, the only person who could approach God was the High Priest, and he could enter the Holy of Holies only once a year and not without blood, to offer sacrifices that would cover the sins of the people. Now that Jesus came and died for our sins, taking our place, we can approach God with boldness and confidence because the bridge between God and man that had been destroyed has been repaired.

Jesus is the perfect mediator who stands in the gap for mankind. Jesus was the only one who was able to meet all the requirements of the law and was found without spot or blemish, thus becoming the spotless Lamb of God. He succeeded where Adam failed. Jesus came as a man anointed of the Holy Spirit. He had to draw from God's anointing. We see Jesus praying long before dawn, communing with the Father.

"Let this mind be in you which was also in Christ Jesus, who being in the form of God, did not consider it robbery to be equal with God, but made himself of no reputation, taking the form of a bondservant, and coming in the likeness of men, and being found in appearance as a man, He humbled Himself and became obedient to the point of death, even the death of the cross" (Philippians 2:5–8 NKJV).

The Bible tells us that Jesus humbled Himself. He became obedient even unto death. He did it all for us. He identified with man so that He could fully represent man to God. Jesus was a man of prayer. He spent much time in prayer, drawing from the wisdom of His Father. Jesus was subject to temptation just as we are, but He never gave in to it. He had a body that was subject to temptation. He is able to relate to us now because He knows man's weakness. He has become our merciful and faithful High Priest, representing us to the Father. He identified with us so that we, through the new birth, could identify with Him.

Jesus walked in total victory at all times. The Devil could not overcome Him. He had to do what we couldn't do. He walked in righteousness uncontaminated by sin. Everything had to be done legally because God is a just God, else He could not be our representative.

He represented us in life, and He represented us in death. It wasn't until Jesus overcame death that humanity was set free and death lost its grip on mankind. Jesus living a perfect life wasn't enough to pay for the sins of mankind. He had to also represent us in death and triumph over it. He had to break the power of death over mankind. The Bible tells us in Hebrews 2:15 that man was in bondage all his lifetime because of the fear of death. Jesus took the sting out of death and removed the fear of it.

He became our perfect substitute in His life, His death, and His resurrection, thus paying the penalty. That is why we now live for Him. That is the reason we have victory over sin in our life and are able to live a victorious life. That is why when we come to Jesus as newborn babies we require the milk of the Word to grow by. Later on, we move on to the meat of the Word. The Word of God is what changes the way we think and the way we act. It's the Word of God that is needed in our life to build that firm foundation that cannot be shaken.

Chapter 2 Questions

1. God sees you seated with _____.
2. We must change how we act, how we respond, and how we _____.
3. To grow up in Christ, we must first understand the _____ of the old nature.
4. We couldn't _____ ourselves because of the old nature.
5. The road leading to life is _____ and _____.
6. God gave man the ability to make _____.
7. Christian growth is _____.
8. The Bible is our _____.
9. We must _____ our mind with the Word of God.
10. _____ are containers of _____ or life.

Chapter 2 suggested Bible reading

Ephesians 2:4–6
Ephesians 2:1–3
Matthew 7:13
Matthew 18:28
Romans 12:1–2
Proverbs 18:21

Chapter 2 Answers

1. God see you seated with Christ.
2. We must change how we act, how we respond and how we speak.
3. To grow up in Christ we must first understand the characteristics of the old nature.
4. We couldn't change ourselves because of the old nature.
5. The road leading to life is narrow and compacted
6. God gave man the ability to make choices.
7. Christian growth is progressive
8. The Bible is our guidebook.
9. We must renew our mind with the Word of God
10. Words are containers of death or life.

Chapter 3

The Three P's of Positive Change

We are creatures of habit. We don't like change; we like staying in our comfort zone. As Christians, we must choose change. Change requires a change of direction. Where we once walked on the path that led to destruction, we now walk on the path that leads to life.

Three Stages of Christian Growth

There are three stages of Christian growth. The first is positional change. Positional change took place when you made Jesus the Lord of your life. Your position changed: you went from death to life, from darkness to light. You were taken out of the kingdom of darkness and translated into the kingdom of light. The sin nature was taken out of you, and you were given a new nature. Now you are to consider the old man or old nature dead, take off the old man, and put on the new man or the new nature, which is created in righteousness. You were a sinner, but now you have become a new creation in Christ. You are no longer the person you used to be with the old desires and habits of the flesh. You are now what the Bible calls the new man.

Then there is progressive change. All of us are at the place of progressive change. It doesn't matter how long we have been Christians; we are still progressing in our walk with the Lord. We are being changed from glory to glory. God is doing a work in us day after day, developing it, perfecting it, and bringing it to full completion. The Bible tells us that God is working in you; He is energizing and creating in you the power and the desire to will and to work for Him. He's not just putting a desire in you. With the desire He is giving you the energy and the power to do something with the desires He has placed within your heart. Progressive change means that there is a progression of change that began when you were born again and will continue until the day Jesus comes back and gives you your new body, which will be changed.

The last change we are going to see is permanent change. That will take place when these mortal bodies will have put on immortality and we will be forever changed. 1 Corinthians 15: 51-54. Our bodies are now subject to sickness and disease, decay and death, but one day this mortal is going to put on immortality and we will all be changed in a moment, in the twinkling of an eye. That is when our redemption will be complete.

Your spirit received an instant transformation at the new birth, and the Lord has given you the Holy Spirit as a down payment of the redemption of your body. None of us has the fullness of the Spirit because these mortal bodies cannot stand it. We have a portion of His spirit, and when we come together, we see a greater portion.

Now we see through a glass darkly, but then we will see face-to-face. One day we will know Him even as He is known. That change begins when we continue in God's Word, and it becomes a part of us through spending time in His presence in prayer. When Moses returned from spending forty days and nights in the presence of God, the people couldn't look upon his face, because the glory of God was all over him and he didn't even know it. The more time we spend with God, the more we draw closer to Him, the more of Him we are going to have, and the more we are being conformed into His image.

Change Is a Choice

Change is a way of life. Everything around us is constantly changing, and we have to accustom ourselves to change. The choice we have to make is to let go of our old lifestyle and change it for one that is pleasing to the Lord. We have to choose to change the old mind-sets and renew our mind daily with the Word of God. Change is a choice. You must choose to change and to allow God to show you which areas of your life need change.

Every person whom God called had to make the choice to change. The fishermen had to leave their fishing nets and follow Him. The tax collector had to leave his position to follow Jesus. Abraham had to leave his kinfolk behind and go to a place with unfamiliar faces and surroundings to follow God. Many times it's the familiar surroundings and people that are taking our attention away from the things of God. Each one of these people had to make a decision to obey God or stay in their comfort zone. We will never know what God has in store for us until we step out of our comfort zone and make changes. There's a saying that goes, "If you don't like the results you're getting, change what you're doing." We want things to change without changing what we're doing, and it's not going to happen.

When temptation comes our way, we have to make a choice. We have the choice of giving in or taking the way of escape, of becoming discouraged because of the way things are or encouraging ourselves in the Lord. We can choose to let the tests and trials of life make us bitter or better. We can see them as stumbling blocks or stepping-stones. Change is required if we want God's best. God is not asking us to change in our own ability; He has given us His Spirit, His grace, and His Word to help us change. God knows the condition of mankind and how he thinks. God gave us His Word to be our GPS on the road of life.

One thing that requires definite change in us is our character. What do I mean when I say our character requires change? Christ in us must make a difference that the world can see. All of us have character traits that we have picked up throughout the years. Some are good and some are bad. Some of those character traits are our strong points, and some are our weak points. As we grow in the Word, we begin to find out what is pleasing to God and what isn't. The Bible teaches us what we have to do to improve our strong points and how we can strengthen our weak points. As we get into the Word, we begin to see ourselves as God sees us. The way we see ourselves is a result of what we believe about ourselves.

Many people grow up believing that they can never amount to anything and can't succeed at anything. They believe they are failures. Your mind-set about yourself has to change so that you begin to see yourself as God sees you. God sees you victorious, as more than a conqueror, as prosperous and loved. God wants you to succeed in life. Your attitude about life is what determines your success or your failure. Attitude is the mental and emotional response to the circumstances of life. You must choose to have purpose and goals for your life. God is ready to help you make the necessary changes when you are ready to make them.

The Bible teaches us to put off the old man, or old nature, and be clothed with the new man. The old nature is the part that ruled your thoughts, reasoning, and emotions before you came to the Lord. You now have a new nature, but you have to grow into it. Putting off the old man is a choice one has to make.

There is no excuse for remaining unchanged after becoming a Christian; everything that's needed to make proper change has been provided for you. The changes you make are going to benefit you, and they are going to benefit others as well. You are the one who is going to benefit most from the changes you make. Then you can be a blessing to others.

If you read Ephesians 4:22–32, you'll find that certain things are required of you as you endeavor to live the new life. First you must put off your former conversation, the way you used to talk, the negative words you used to speak, and the lying. Your nature has changed, so your old lifestyle has to change. The Bible says to be angry and sin not. It doesn't say we should never be angry; we just shouldn't allow our anger to cause us to sin. The reason we should not allow our anger to cause us to sin is that it opens the door to the Devil. The Bible tells us not to give place to the Devil. Anger can be learned by association. If you hang around an angry person, you will learn his ways without realizing what you're doing. (Proverbs 22:24 NKJV) says, "Make no friendship with an angry man and with a furious man do not go: lest you learn his ways and set a snare to thy soul." You can easily become ensnared by your emotions when you allow your emotions to get out of control. When we are easily angered, that anger begins to dictate our actions. Anger will affect you more than it does the one at whom it is aimed. We are not to let corrupt communication come out of our mouth, and we are not to grieve the Holy Spirit.

The Bible teaches that our body is the temple of the Holy Spirit, who dwells in us. We should always be conscious of the Holy Spirit's presence in our life. The Bible says we are to let all bitterness, wrath, anger, clamor, and evil speaking be put away from us. We are to be kind one to another, tenderhearted and forgiving one another even as God for Christ's sake has forgiven us. (Ephesians 4:22-32) God doesn't remember your sins or past mistakes. God reminds you of who you are, not who you were.

The Bible contains instructions that show us how to live. One cannot go through life without direction, goals, or vision. Vision propels one forward, and goals keep one focused. Jesus came to earth with a goal He had to accomplish. If He had not accomplished what He came to do, you and I would still be lost in sin. When He was on the cross at the most crucial time in

His life, He was able to stay focused on the results of what He was about to accomplish. He was thinking of you and me and all the many others who would have the opportunity to become children of God. The Bible says in Hebrews 12:2 "Looking unto Jesus, the author and finisher of our faith, who for the joy that was set before Him endured the cross, despising the shame and has sat down at the right hand of the throne of God." It took courage and determination to hang on that cross wounded and bleeding. Even though impending death was before Him, His goal would not let Him quit. He saw through the ages the many that would accept His sacrifice and be born again.

The Bible tells us that God has good plans for us and not plans for evil. (Jeremiah 29:11) We can trust God with our life because He is the author of life. Doesn't it make sense to follow the manufacturer's guidebook if we want the best results possible? The Word of God is nourishment to our whole being. We can take in the Word of God daily and receive the life of God in our spirit, and it will ultimately change the outside. The only way one can become acquainted with God is to spend time studying and meditating in the Word and spending time in communion with Him. When you study the life of Christ and His teachings, you find life because the Word of God is life.

"My son, give attention to my words; Incline your ear to my sayings. Do not let them depart from your eyes; keep them in the midst of your heart; for they are life to those who find them, and health to all their flesh" (Proverbs 4:20–22 NKJV).

God's words are life to those who find them, and health to all their flesh. They are not only containers of life but givers of life.

Three *P*'s of Positive Change Review

1. Positional change: When you were born again, you went from death to life. Your position changed; you are no longer a sinner. The wages of sin that hung over your

head have been paid in full. God is now your heavenly Father. You have been bought with a price; you are not your own. Before coming to the Lord, you were following the course of this world, but now that you have made Jesus the Lord of your life, your destiny has changed. You are now walking on the straight and narrow road that leads to life.

2. Progressive change: You are now being changed from glory to glory. Your life is being transformed as you read the Word and meditate on it. Your life is being changed daily as you renew your mind with the Word of God; you are being conformed into the image of Christ.

3. Permanent change: This change occurs when these mortal bodies put on immortality. The Bible tells us that we will be changed in the twinkling of an eye. Our bodies will be changed into spiritual bodies that never die.

Chapter 3 Questions and Things to Think About

1. How many stages of Christian growth are there?
2. Name the three stages of Christian growth.
3. What is meant by positional change?
4. What is meant by progressive change?
5. What is meant by permanent change?
6. _____ is a way of life
7. _____ is a choice.
8. Tests and trials can be used as _____ or _____.
9. Whom do the changes you make benefit?
10. God has a _____ for your life.

Chapter 3 suggested Bible reading

Jeremiah 29:11
2 Corinthians 3:18

Chapter 3 Answers

1. There are three stages of Christian growth.
2. The three stages of Christian growth are positional change, progressive change, and permanent change.
3. Positional change took place when you made Jesus the Lord of your life. You went from death to life and from darkness to light.
4. Progressive change is the progress you make day by day as you walk with the Lord and grow in the Word.
5. Permanent change takes place when these mortal bodies put on immortality; it is the last stage of growth we will see.
6. Change is a way of life.
7. Change is a choice.
8. Tests and trials can be used as stepping-stones or stumbling blocks.
9. You benefit from the changes you make.
10. God has a plan for your life.

Chapter 4

It Is Finished

What are we talking about when we say it is finished? When one says it's finished, it means it's complete, it's done, and it's been accomplished. Nothing else has to be done.

"When Jesus therefore had received the sour wine, He said, 'It is finished!' and bowing his head, He gave up His spirit" (John 19:30 NKJV).

A finished work was done through Jesus' life, death, burial, resurrection, and ascension. There is nothing lacking, and nothing needs to be added to improve it. The sooner we understand this, the easier it will be to take the Word of God literally. It is human nature for us to think one has to do something to help God out. It's difficult for human beings to think that Jesus did something without their help. Man thinks he has to work for his salvation, to do something for God to love him, or to do something to be accepted or approved by God. There is nothing more you have to do. God has already accepted you. He knew you before you were born. He knows everything about you. He even knows when you get up in the morning and when you go to bed; moreover, He knows what's on your tongue even before you speak it.

The first thing we want to look at is the fact that when Jesus finished what He came to do, He sat down at the right hand of God. The work was finished. He didn't have to work anymore, He didn't have to suffer anymore, and the work He came to do was finished. When we come to Him and receive Him as our Lord and Savior, we become new creatures in Christ. Our new life begins the moment we are born again. Everything one receives from God must be received by faith, by trusting God and taking Him at His word.

Second Corinthians 5:17 says, "Therefore if anyone is in Christ, he is a new creation: old things have passed away; behold all things are become new."

When we were born again, we received the life of God. We became new creatures that had never existed before. You might be thinking, I can't see any difference. That is because the difference begins in your spirit, where you received a new nature, the nature of God. Then as you begin to study the Word of God and learn how to apply it to your daily life, you will begin to see a big difference in the way you think, the way you talk, and the way you act. It's not going to happen right away, because as we said earlier, change is progressive.

Maybe you will face temporary rejection from friends and family because they don't understand what has taken place. When my husband and I received the Lord, we found ourselves alienated from friends and family we used to be around all the time. We didn't understand what was going on, but it was the best thing that ever happened to us because it gave us time to grow in the Lord and in the Word. The natural mind doesn't understand the things of the spirit. People might make fun of you and call you names, but you're going to find that when they need help or answers, they are going to come looking for you. You will learn to see yourself as God sees you and not as people see you.

When I was born again, there were areas in me that needed change. I was a shy, intimidated person. I had low self-esteem and compared myself with others. I was afraid to say anything because I thought people weren't interested in what I had to say. I lived in a prison of my own making, afraid of rejection and disapproval. I thought disapproval or disagreement meant people were rejecting me as a person. The Word of God is what began to change the way I saw myself. As I studied the Word, I began to see myself as a person of importance because God loves me. I found I didn't have to compare myself with others because there is no one else like me. I am unique, just the way God wanted me to be. I was able to accept myself as a person of worth. Many times one sees oneself through the eyes of circumstances in one's life instead of through the finished work of Christ.

Character traits were developed in you through the company you kept, the way your parents raised you, and the things they taught you. Fear of different things was instilled in you. God's Word teaches that we were created in the image of God. When Adam and Eve sinned, sin began to mar that image until man could not see himself as God saw him. There are good points and bad points in everyone. The Word teaches us to build on our strong points and to minimize the weak points. Where I was once afraid of my own shadow, now I am courageous because the Bible tells me that the righteous are bold as a lion. We will discuss righteousness later on. Righteousness is what God clothed you in when you received Jesus as your Lord and Savior—not your righteousness but His.

People might see you as a coward or a weakling because you no longer do the things you used to do. People don't understand the change in you. They don't understand that it takes courage to admit you are a sinner and especially to admit you need help. It takes courage to go against the flow when everyone else is going in the opposite direction; it's much easier to follow the crowd. The Word of God instills courage, confidence, and boldness in you.

Fear will keep you bound. There are different kinds of fear, but they all hinder your spiritual progress. There's the fear of the unknown, fear of change, fear of what people are going to say, fear of losing friends, and many other kinds of fear. The Devil works through fear just as God works through faith. We will discuss faith in a later chapter and discuss it in such a way that you can learn to walk in faith and not in fear. The Devil lies to you and tells you that you can't do anything anymore, that you're giving up too much, and that if you become a Christian, you won't have any fun anymore. He is operating in fear because he doesn't want to lose you. Your new lifestyle requires change.

Your problems don't end when you become a believer; they've just begun because now you have an enemy who would like nothing more than to destroy God's plan for your life. There's comfort in knowing you're not alone. The Lord is with you to help you every step of the way, and other Christians are there to help you grow.

Jeremiah 31:34 says, "No more shall every man teach his neighbor, and every man his brother, saying, 'know the Lord,' for they all shall know me, from the least of them to the greatest of them, says the Lord. For I will forgive their iniquity, and their sin I will remember no more."

This doesn't mean that you don't need teachers. We saw in an earlier chapter that God placed teachers in the church for the perfecting of the saints for the work of the ministry. The passage from Jeremiah is saying that we all have the ability to know the Lord for ourselves, unlike the children of Israel who were afraid of God. The High Priest used to go into the Holy of Holies to present sacrifices for the sins of the people every year, but those sacrifices could never erase their sins. They could cover them only for a year. Your sins are forgiven forever. God doesn't remember them anymore.

Since you are now a new creature, God sees you through the shed blood of His Son. He no longer sees you as a sinner. He not only forgets your sin and iniquity but will never remember them or bring them up again.

Isaiah 44:22 says, "I have blotted out, like a thick cloud, your transgressions, and like a cloud, your sins, return to me, for I have redeemed you."

Redemption means "to buy back." Earlier we talked about how Jesus had to come born of a virgin without the sin nature in order to redeem mankind. We talked about how sin had separated us from the life of God and how Jesus paid the price required to purchase our redemption. Thank God for His mercy, His love, and His grace. He has blotted out our sin as a thick cloud.

We're talking about what God has done. It is finished; it's a finished work that doesn't require anything added to it. There's nothing that you or I have to do to be accepted. We are already accepted in Christ as if we had never sinned.

Psalm 103:12 says, "As far as the east is from the west, So far has he removed our transgressions from us."

God has removed your transgressions as far as the east is from the west. No matter how far east you go, you will always be traveling east. East and west never meet. If you're traveling west, you will always be traveling west unless you change direction. You can look for your lost sins, but you're not going to find them, because as far as God is concerned, they no longer exist. Oh yes, the enemy will try to remind you of them, but once you know what God did with your sins, you can let the devil know that you know they no longer exist, that you are redeemed and a new creature in Christ.

Many Christians live in torment over their past because they have not received the revelation of the finished work of Christ. The enemy is able to torment them with their past and bring them under condemnation, which causes them to live in guilt over sins that have already been forgiven and forgotten.

We need to know not only who God is but who our enemy is. The Bible says, in reference to the enemy, that the thief comes to kill, to steal, and to destroy. That seems simple enough when we learn to distinguish the difference between what gives life and what destroys. God is blamed for many things that He has nothing to do with. The enemy's only strategy is to kill, steal, and destroy, and he doesn't care how he does it or who he uses to do it. If he can succeed at keeping you from receiving the revelation of who you are, in Christ, then he can keep you bound to your past. God wants you to succeed and to live an abundant life.

"And you, being dead in your trespasses and the uncircumcision of your flesh, he has made alive together with Him, having forgiven you all trespasses, having wiped out the handwriting of requirements that was against us, which was contrary to us. He has taken it out of the way, having nailed it to the cross" (Colossians 2:13–14 NKJV).

He blotted out the handwriting that was against you and nailed your sins to the cross. Your sins have been forgiven. God is no longer holding anything against you. Whatever you've done in the past is forgiven and forgotten. The times you failed, the times you missed it, and the things you tried to hide from God have no effect on you now that you are a new creation in Christ. In Him there are no failures. If we fail, we fail on our own. The only person who fails is the one who falls and refuses to get up again.

We have been reconciled to God through Jesus Christ; we are back in right standing with God, justified by His blood. Now we have access to His presence. He invites us to come boldly to the throne room of grace, where we can find help and grace in our times of need. (Hebrews 4:16) We are no longer separated from God.

God began working in you the moment you were born again. The Bible tells us in Philippians 1:6 that it's a good work and He will bring it to completion. The Amplified Bible tells us that He is developing it and perfecting it and bringing it to full completion in your life. God has a plan that only you can fulfill, but He doesn't expect you to do it alone. He has sent you a helper, the Holy Spirit, the one who reveals the Word to you. Jesus said He would show us things to come and would bring all things to our remembrance of what He has spoken. Jesus said He would not leave us orphans but would send us another comforter who would not only be with us but would be in us. He lives in your spirit; He will lead you and guide you into all truth.

"For we are God's (own) handiwork, (His workmanship), recreated in Christ Jesus, [born anew] that we may do those good works which God predestined (planned beforehand) for us [taking paths that which he prepared ahead of time], that we should walk in them [living the good life which he prearranged and made ready for us to live]" (Ephesians 2:10 AB).

God prepared paths for you to walk in long before you were born again. He planned a good life for you and for me; we just need to follow His plan. As you grow in Christ, you will begin to see many changes take place in your life. Your thoughts, your desires, and the way you see things will begin to change, and you will see a change in the way you respond to others and the way you respond to situations.

What the New Birth Has Done for You

The new birth has made you a child of God. God took you out of the kingdom of darkness and placed you into His kingdom. As a child of God, you have certain rights and privileges. You are no longer separated from the life of God but are now reconciled to Him. You have been made righteous with His righteousness. As a child of God, you have an inheritance. The Bible says that the spirit of God bears witness with your spirit that you are a son of God, an heir of God, and a joint heir with Jesus Christ. If a rich aunt died and left you an inheritance, you would want to find out what that rich aunt left you, wouldn't you? God created all things, and everything belongs to Him: the gold, the silver, the cattle on a thousand hills, everything belongs to Him. Jesus, being God's Son, left us an inheritance when He died for us. Everything that belongs to Jesus belongs to us because we are joint heirs with Him. He shares everything with us: His spirit, His wisdom, His righteousness, and eternal life.

When we think of prosperity, we think of money, but prosperity is more than just money. Money can't buy everything, but faith in God and His wisdom can obtain what money can't buy. Prosperity is not a bad word. God believes in prosperity.

"This book of the law shall not depart from your mouth, but you shall meditate in it day and night, that you may observe to do according to all that is written in it. For then you will make your way prosperous, and then you will have good success" (Joshua 1:8).

There are many prosperous people in this world, but not all of them have good success. Many have spent their lifetime reaching for success and arrive only to find that their heart's craving was not satisfied. The emptiness was still present because worldly success is not what satisfies the heart of man. They have obtained riches and they have obtained things, but they are unhappy, dissatisfied, and lonely. They have found success, but they have lost their peace. God promises to give us good success if we walk in His ways and meditate in His Word day and night. He wants not only for us to meditate in His Word but to become doers of His Word. The only way one can become a doer of the Word is to get wisdom as the Bible says. Knowledge without wisdom puffs up. Knowledge alone can't produce much; it takes wisdom to know how to apply the knowledge one has.

Prosperity is not measured in what money can buy but in whom we know. All true prosperity comes from God. We have good success because we can lie down at night and our sleep is sweet because we have no worries. All of our needs are met according to His riches in glory by Christ Jesus. Prosperity is not measured in dollar amounts. You know you are prospering when you have plenty for yourself, your family, and to share with those who are less fortunate than yourself. Prosperity gives you peace of mind regardless of the state of the economy.

The Bible says God gives us the power to get wealth. He gives us not only the power to get wealth but the wisdom to know what to do with it. If we want good success, we have to do it God's way. The Bible says, "What good is it for a man to gain the world and lose his soul?" The world says, "Hold on to what you have, and keep all you can." Greed is the world's way. God says, "Give and it shall be given unto you." God wants to bless you so that you can be a blessing. There's only one place we find out what our inheritance is and how to obtain it, and that place is in the Bible.

I can't speak for everyone, but I can attest to the fact that God blesses those who love Him and follow Him. My family has been walking with the Lord for thirty-five years, and we have never lacked for anything. Yes, we were pressed for finances sometimes, but God always came through for us. We became tithers immediately, giving our 10 percent to the church, and God has been true to His Word. We started out in poverty, making it from paycheck to paycheck, always in need. We didn't prosper overnight either. We began to prosper as we grew in the Word and renewed our minds to think like God thinks. I can attest to the truth that God prospers those who love Him and that He multiplies the seed they sow.

"Beloved, I pray that you may prosper in all things and be in health, just as your soul prospers" (3 John 1:2 NKJV).

We had to gain knowledge of God's Word and then get wisdom to apply it to our life. We slowly began to see increase in every area of our life, and now we can say God is abundantly blessing us financially. He has given us ideas for witty inventions and increased us to where we now live a very comfortable life. I'm convinced it could not have happened if we had not grown in the Word and put it into practice.

God has provided so much for you and me. Many Christians will never receive their inheritance, not because it wasn't given to them but because they never took the time to study the Word and find out what Jesus provided for them. They never took time to grow and allow their mind to prosper in the Word. It takes diligence, determination, dedication, and hard work to accomplish something.

Chapter 4 Questions

1. What did Jesus mean when He said, "It is finished"?
2. When does change begin?
3. _____ traits were developed through the company we kept, the way we were raised, and the things we were taught.
4. Whose image were you created in?
5. What marred the image we were created in?
6. What does it take to go against the flow when everyone else is going in the opposite direction?
7. _____ is the opposite of faith.
8. What does redemption mean?
9. Why was redemption necessary?
10. Does God keep a record of your sins?
11. When does a person fail?
12. God sent us a helper. Who is he?

Chapter 4 suggested Bible reading

John 19:30
Genesis 1:27
1Timothy 1:7
Colossians 2:13–14
John 14:26

Chapter 4 Answers

1. God's plan was finished; Jesus accomplished what He was sent to do.
2. Change begins the moment you are born again.
3. Character traits were developed through the company we kept, the way we were raised, and the things we were taught.
4. Man was created in the image of God.
5. Sin marred the image we were created in.
6. It takes courage to go against the flow when everyone else is going in the opposite direction.
7. Fear is the opposite of faith.
8. The word redemption means "to buy back."
9. Redemption was necessary because man had been sold under sin.
10. God said He will remember your sins no more.
11. A person fails when he refuses to get up again.
12. God sent the Holy Spirit to be our helper.

Chapter 5

Getting Started

How do I begin my life as a new believer?

The first step is to repent of your sins and receive Jesus Christ as your Lord and Savior. What does it mean to repent? It means to be truly sorry for your sins, to have a desire to change your life, and to make a complete turnaround. Change the direction you are going in and follow Jesus. Choose the straight and narrow road Jesus talks about in the Gospels. Once the choice has been made, it's time to get started.

Where do I start?

When I was born again, I immediately lost my desire for worldly things. I didn't have any major addictions. I didn't try drugs, but I did like dancing and certain kinds of music. I had a collection of albums by artists I admired, but suddenly they were not important to me anymore. My heart had a new love, a new hunger, and I followed my heart. The only thing that satisfied that hunger was getting to know the Lord and learning all I could about Him.

I recommend you start by reading the Bible because it is God's instruction book for your life. It is God's Word to you, and in it you will find out what Jesus did for you and how to live a life that is pleasing to Him.

Which version of the Bible is the best one?

There are several versions. Some are easier to understand than others. I recommend you use one that you can understand clearly. Most preachers use the King James Version, which is not the easiest to understand. If you understand that the Word of God is inspired by the Holy Spirit, you will find that all versions that teach that Jesus is the only way to heaven say basically the same thing. Some versions are easier to read because they're in modern-day language, and others amplify certain words to give the Word greater meaning without changing the content. The New King James Version is easier to understand than the older version. I use the Amplified Bible in some of my studies because it gives a wider meaning to Scripture, but I would not recommend it as a starter Bible. You need something you can understand.

Many Christians take their Bible to church on Sunday and then place it on the shelf the rest of the week, where it gathers dust; it cannot help one change if one doesn't read what's written therein. The Word of God is the living Word. It's alive because it contains life, and the more you read it, the more you understand God's plan, will, and purpose for your life. No, you're not going to understand it right away, but Jesus said, "If you abide in My Word, you are my disciples indeed. And you shall know the truth, and the truth will make you free." (John 8:31-32 NKJV) The Word of God has the power not only to make you free but to keep you free. The Bible is called the word of truth.

The Bible says in Mark 4 that the sower sows the Word. What does that mean? It means that the Word of God is seed. It must be planted in the soil of your heart. Once it's planted, it must be cared for. The way we care for the soil is by keeping our heart from being contaminated by other things. There are many things that contaminate our heart so that the Word of God cannot produce. There is nothing wrong with the Word. The Word of God is incorruptible seed; that means it will always produce when planted in good soil.

In reading the fourth chapter of Mark, you find that Jesus is telling a parable about the seed that He later interprets for His disciples. He speaks about the different types of soil where the Word is sown. He compares the first type of soil with a new believer. The new believer hears the Word, but Satan comes immediately to take away the seed that was sown in his heart. How does Satan do it? He does it by distractions and other things. Satan doesn't want to give the Word time to put down roots because he knows that if it puts down roots, it has a better chance of producing.

The part of the parable in which other seed falls on stony ground is also about new believers. They hear and receive the Word with gladness, but they have no root in themselves. They endure for a while, but when the tests and trials of life come, they are offended. When one is first born again, everything is new and exciting, but the excitement wears off, and the tests and trials come to take away the Word that was sown in their heart.

The parable talks of another type of ground, or people: they hear the Word, but the cares of this world and the deceitfulness of riches and lusts for other things enter in and choke the Word so that it becomes unfruitful. Many Christians start out well but get caught up in the things going on around them, and if they don't continue in the Word, the Word that is in them gets choked by the cares of this world. There is nothing wrong with the seed; it's the ground that determines if the seed is going to produce thirty-, sixty, or a hundredfold. When the seed falls on good ground, those people hear the Word and receive it and bring forth fruit up to a hundredfold.

We know that if we want to plant a garden, the seed must be planted in good soil because if there are rocks underneath, they will hinder the growth of the plant. The ground must be taken care of because if the ground is producing weeds and thorns, they will choke the plant and it cannot produce a good harvest. In West Texas, we have trouble with the wind and not getting enough rain. Because it's dry farming, farmers depend on rain for a cotton harvest. If there is not enough rain, the seed can't break through the hard ground, and if it comes up, it dies quickly.

We have a vacation home in Missouri. Our house is on a hill in the Ozarks. There is a beautiful view from every window in the house. In order to plant grass, we had to put down several layers of soil first because it's all rock underneath. The rock does not allow the seed to put down roots deep enough to sustain the life of the plant. If the soil of our heart is not prepared, it cannot produce good fruit, because it doesn't have enough depth for the seed to grow.

You're going to find that once you begin to apply the Word to your life—once you begin to act on what the Word says and once it becomes a part of you—your life will begin to change. Your eyes will be opened and your understanding will be enlightened, and you will realize where the other road was leading you. You will begin to see other things you didn't see before because of your blindness. Your understanding will become enlightened; you will understand things you never understood before.

You are going to have to find out what works best for you. Many Bible scholars suggest you begin reading the gospels of Matthew, Mark, Luke, and John. I agree it's a good place to start, but I've also found that many people who are not familiar with the Bible get confused when they start with the first chapter of Matthew because it contains the genealogy of Jesus Christ. Because it's hard to understand, they never attempt to go beyond that. The genealogy is outlined in verses 1 to 17; you might find it interesting to know who God used to bring forth our Lord and Savior Jesus Christ into this world. It's a good place to familiarize oneself with the Word of God.

All of God's Word is important because every book in the Bible points to Jesus—even the stories. Throughout the Bible, you will find new insight into God's plan and purpose for mankind. Each writer is unique in that the Holy Spirit inspired each one to write according to his personality and each book was written as each writer was able to see and understand what the spirit of God was saying to each one individually.

All four gospels contain some of the same information given from different perspectives of how each author saw and understood things. All four gospels are great tools to help you begin your journey of faith. You might become interested in a certain subject. When that happens, many Bibles have references on those subjects to help you get a clearer picture. All you have to do is find the reference for that certain Word or passage and look it up. You will find that most Bibles have the words of Jesus in red. You will find out how Jesus related to His disciples and taught them, and how He taught the people whenever He had an opportunity. He used many illustrations, parables, and comparisons to make it easier for the common people to understand what He was saying.

Some suggest you begin in the gospel of John because John had a close relationship with the Lord and talks a lot about love and how Jesus loved us. I find each gospel of great value to any reader. By comparing them, we see before us a bigger picture of what Jesus came to do and the instructions He left to His followers.

It's important that you understand the written Word of God because it contains spiritual food for your spirit. Just as you need food to sustain your physical life, you need spiritual food to grow spiritually. It is nourishment to your spirit and is profitable in developing your spirit man to be more Christ-like.

The Bible says faith comes by hearing and hearing by the Word of God. The more one hears the Word, the more faith comes, but one can't have faith if there is no Word. As you read the Word, you will become acquainted with Jesus and learn how to communicate with God. Communication with your heavenly Father is of great importance in your spiritual growth. He is the one who meets all of our needs; He is the one who has given us everything we need to live a successful life and to become productive Christians in His kingdom, so prayer must become an essential part of your Christian walk.

Prayer

The four gospels give us the basics of how to pray according to the Word of God. Many of us were brought up in churches where we were taught to pray to certain "saints" or to go in prayer through Mary to God. Please let me make it clear that I am in no way putting down any denomination; I myself was brought up in one of those denominations, I can only say what I see in the Word of God. The Bible teaches that there is only one mediator between God and man, and that is *Jesus Christ.* When He accomplished the work His Father sent Him to do, He ascended into heaven and is seated at the right hand of God, making intercession to God for us. Because He humbled Himself and was obedient unto death, God highly exalted Him and gave Him the name above all names that at the name of Jesus every knee shall bow and every tongue must confess that Jesus Christ is Lord. That name is the only name we can come to God through and the only name that will bring results from our prayers.

God is always listening to the prayers of His children, but there are certain principles of prayer in the Word of God that we must apply to get results. It's said that prayer moves the hand of God, but it has to be done right. Much of the praying done consists of begging God to do something, to change something, or to make something happen. The Bible tells us we can come boldly to the throne of grace to obtain, not to beg. Now that you are born again, you are a child of God and have access to God by the Holy Spirit. It's important to know the Word of God because in it, we find our answers, and when we pray, we can go to the Father with the promises of God and know that He will answer because He said He would. God looks after His Word to perform it.

Many of these things are taught in church, so church must become an essential part of your Christian walk also. The reason church is important is that God has placed ministers in the church who will help you grow, answer questions, and be there when you need them. We all need one another. There is no such thing as a Lone Ranger in the kingdom of God. I've seen many Christians go off on their own and become prey for the enemy. The enemy is like a wolf that waits in hiding until he sees the little lamb stray from the flock and then goes in for the kill. Most of the animal kingdom does the same thing. An animal of prey waits until its victim is at its most vulnerable state.

"Be sober, be vigilant; because your adversary the devil walks about like a roaring lion, seeking whom he may devour: Resist him steadfast in the faith, knowing that the same sufferings are experienced by your brotherhood in the world" (1 Peter 5:8–9NKJV).

As long as you stay in fellowship with God's people, there will be less chance for the enemy to catch you off guard. You must keep your guard up at all times and leave no place for the enemy to get in.

Get Involved

Get involved in your local church. Do whatever there is to do according to your ability. Getting involved helps you get to know people in the church and helps you grow faster. I believe people grow up faster when they become involved. We see folks all the time who have been in church for forty years and have never gotten involved, and there is very little growth seen in them. God is pleased when we do whatever our hand finds to do and we do it as unto the Lord, without murmuring or complaining.

Yes, God expects us to go to church when we are born again, but that alone is not what pleases God. Growth and change are what pleases God. Being faithful in your local church is pleasing to your heavenly Father. Faithfulness is what He looks for when He's looking for someone to promote. The Bible says all promotion comes from God. The more things we get involved in, the more we are able to see a greater scope of what ministry is all about. You will find that it's easier to find your place when you get involved in different areas of the ministry. The pulpit is not the ultimate thing. Every kind of worker is needed in the church and is equally important; the ministry can't run without volunteers. Many Christians today are like fish out of water. They don't seem to fit in anywhere, and they become church hoppers, going from one church to another looking for their place, never satisfied in any one place because they have no stability. Faithfulness is the key to finding your place in the body of Christ and the only way that you are going to find true peace.

Many of us started out cleaning bathrooms, helping in the nursery, helping with the children, door greeting or ushering, or even working in the parking lot before we got to the pulpit. Not everyone is called to a pulpit ministry, but we are all called to the ministry of helps. We are all called to share the good news of the gospel of Jesus Christ. Whenever you share the gospel, you're going to find that not everyone is going to be receptive. Don't take it personally. It's not up to you to save them; it's your job to share the Word of salvation and the Holy Spirit's job to convict them of their sin and save them. It was such a relief when I found out that I can't save anyone and that I don't have to convince anyone; it's not my job but the Holy Spirit's. Yeah, you will have an opportunity to become offended, but if you understand that your part is to share the gospel of Jesus Christ and you do it well, with a sincere heart, you can leave satisfied that you did your job and that it's up to God to do the rest.

Don't let anyone tell you that when you become a Christian, you can't do anything, you can't have any fun, and you can't enjoy life. This is the real life. This is the life Jesus died to give us. Everything else leads to destruction, and sooner or later the wages of sin must be paid. Jesus wants you to live the abundant life that He paid for with His blood. Everything you will ever need He has already provided for you. As you grow and mature in the Word, you will find out how to obtain the promises of God. There is no greater life than the Christian life. There is no joy greater than serving God.

Preparing for the Race

We can learn some valuable lessons from athletes, from how they train and discipline their bodies for the purpose of winning in the sport they are involved in. They train daily and discipline themselves in what they eat, in exercise, in practice, in temperance, and in character. Why? If they don't train themselves, they could fumble the ball, they could give up before the race is over, or they could miss the mark and be disqualified. Not only do they strictly discipline themselves but they clothe themselves with the proper clothing for the game they are involved in.

How does this compare with the race we Christians are in? The race we are involved in requires strict training in order to be a good soldier in the army of God and to run the race well that is set before us. We also have to clothe ourselves with the new nature and put off the old. The Bible calls it putting off the old man and putting on the new. We can compare ourselves to an Olympic runner. If the Olympic runner doesn't wear proper clothing for the race, he is going to be hindered from running freely. When we are born again, God clothes us in His righteousness. If we try to run this spiritual race in our own righteousness, we are going to be very much hindered from running a good race, with the consequences of maybe not finishing the race we are called to run.

We all want to hear "Well done" at the end of our race, but we have to run according to the rules.

Chapter 5 Questions

1. The Bible is the _____ book for your life.
2. Which Bible version is most read and preached from?
3. The Word of God is called the living Word because it contains _____.
4. The _____ are a good place to begin reading the Bible.
5. _____ are good because they point you to other Scriptures on the same subject.
6. The Word of God contains _____ for your spirit.
7. _____ with your heavenly Father is of great importance to your spiritual growth.
8. We pray to the Father in the name of _____.
9. _____ must become an essential part of your Christian walk.
10. Get _____ in your local church.

Chapter 5 suggested Bible reading

Hebrews 4:12
1 Peter 2:2
John 16:23

Chapter 5 Answers

1. The Bible is the instruction book for your life.
2. The King James Version is the version most read and preached from.
3. The Word of God is called the living Word because it contains life.
4. The Gospels are a good place to begin reading the Bible.
5. References are good because they point you to other Scriptures on the same subject.
6. The Word of God contains spiritual food for your spirit.
7. Communication with your heavenly Father is of great importance to your spiritual growth.
8. We pray to the Father in the name of Jesus.
9. Church must become an essential part of your Christian walk.
10. Get involved in your local church.

Chapter 6

Equipped to Run

God has set a race before you that you must run until you reach the finish line, but He didn't leave you without equipment to run the race. He gave you the Word of God that will equip you to run this race well. I want you to become like an Olympic runner. I want to have a part in equipping you, training you, and teaching you discipline so that you can overcome every obstacle and reach the finish line without fainting.

The apostle Paul was at one time a Pharisee named Saul and well trained by the best teachers of his day. He believed that it was his calling in life to persecute Christians because he believed they were teaching heresy. He had both men and women hauled off to prison, even consenting to their death, but one day as he was on his way to bring in more Christians, something happened that completely turned his life around and blew his doctrine out of the water.

As he journeyed to Damascus, the Lord Jesus met him and he was never the same again. Everyone who has an encounter with Jesus Christ is changed. (Acts 9)

The Bible gives the accounts not only of great men of God and how they were used of God, but of their faults and shortcomings so that we don't get the idea that God uses only perfect men and women. If we think God can use only perfect people, it will hinder us in our race because not one of us is perfect. We're on our way to perfection, but we haven't arrived yet.

Saul became the great apostle Paul, one of my heroes, who wrote most of the New Testament and has much to say about this spiritual race we are running. One thing I like about Paul is the fact that once he had an encounter with the Lord Jesus Christ, he never turned back. He entered the race and kept running until he reached the finish line. Don't think he didn't have obstacles in his life. He was persecuted, shipwrecked, beaten, stoned, and left for dead, but he didn't let those things stop him. He had his eyes on the prize of the high calling of God in Christ Jesus. That's why he said, "Brethren, I do not count myself to have apprehended; but one thing I do, forgetting those things which are behind and reaching forward to those things which are ahead, I press toward the goal for the prize of the upward call of God in Christ Jesus" (Philippians 3:13–14 NKJV).

You are going to encounter many obstacles in your race, which is why you need training in the Word of God. You need to be able to overcome every obstacle and run your race to the finish line. Our problems don't end just because we receive the Lord Jesus as our Lord and Savior. In fact, the moment you begin running your race, the enemy is going to try to take you out. He knows that if you begin strong, with a firm foundation, it is going to be much harder to trip you up. As long as there is breath in you, he is going to be on your case, so you have to keep your guard up at all times; you have to recognize your enemy and stand your ground. The Bible tells us in (John 10:10) that the thief, the Devil, comes to kill, to steal, and to destroy. That is his mode of operation. You'd think it would be simple enough to recognize the enemy at work, but many Christians still blame other people, their job, their circumstances, the economy, and even God, never zeroing in on the real cause of their problems.

The apostle Paul tells us to keep our eyes fixed on the goal, to forget what lies behind and reach for what lies ahead. God has a wonderful life planned for you, but it's not going to come to you; you must reach for it, you must want it, and you must fight for it. The work has already been done. It's up to you and me to take hold of the finished work of Christ and run with it. How far you want to get in life is up to you. We have each been given the same race to run. Some will run till they cross the finish line, and others will fall by the wayside. I'm not saying that as you run you're not going to trip up and fall every now and then, but each time you get up, you'll become stronger. Just like bodily discipline builds muscle and endurance, exercising the Word of God builds stamina, endurance, and spiritual muscle.

"Therefore we also, since we are surrounded by so great a cloud of witnesses, let us lay aside every weight, and the sin which so easily ensnares us, and let us run with endurance the race that is set before us, looking unto Jesus, the author and the finisher of our faith, who for the joy that was set before Him endured the cross, despising the shame, and has sat down at the right hand of the throne of God" (Hebrews 12:1–2 NKJV).

In the passage above, the writer of Hebrews is telling us to keep our eyes fixed on Jesus; He is the author and the finisher of our faith. Jesus had you and me in mind when He came to pay the price for our redemption. We were the joy that was set before Him, we were the reason He endured the pain and the cross and is now seated at the right hand of God, highly exalted and given a name above all names. It wasn't an easy task He came to do. He endured more pain and suffering than any man who ever lived, and He did it all for you and me. He left His home on high to come here to run a race just like you and me, and He finished it and was able to say, "It is finished." His race wasn't without tests, trials, and temptations, for the Bible tells us that He was tempted in all points as we are, yet was without sin. (Hebrews 4:15) Right at the beginning of His ministry, (Luke 4) the Devil came in to try to make Him quit before He got going. He thought Jesus was going to be an easy target just like Eve, but he wasn't counting on combat with a man who had fasted and prayed in communion with God for forty days and forty nights—a man who had a vision. The Bible tells us that after Jesus returned unto Jordan, He returned in the power of the Spirit. He had overcome the temptations of the enemy and came forth with power. Immediately after that, He began His ministry, a ministry empowered by the Holy Spirit.

You don't have even the slightest idea what God has planned for you. All you know is that you have begun a spiritual race. You want to run it well, so you need to know what is required of you to do that and what's required in order to reach the finish line.

It's going to take discipline, dedication, commitment, and humility to run in this race and reach the finish line. We don't want to be like the children of Israel. God delivered them out of slavery with a strong arm and led them through the wilderness to the Promised Land; God had to take them around the long way because they murmured and complained all the way. They were never satisfied. Even though God was with them as a cloud by day to keep them cool and a fire by night for warmth, they always found something that dissatisfied them, so for forty years they circled the same mountain over and over again, or you could say they went around in circles. That's what many Christians do today: they start out strong, but when tests and trials come, they lose their vision and find themselves right back where they started. God wants us to grow up so that we can overcome the tests and trials of life and not fall into the same trap of the enemy over and over again.

What Are Tests For?

When we were in school, we were given tests, not because it was the teacher's intention to fail us, but because she or he wanted to know what we were learning. God uses the tests and trials in our life to see how much we have grown. The reason so many believers are circling the same mountain is that they have not disciplined themselves and learned to overcome. The same tests and trials keep coming to them only because they keep failing the test. When we'd fail in school, we were sometimes given a chance to retake the test and pass it. God gives us many chances to pass the tests we encounter in life; He not only gives us chances but equips us to pass those tests. When you take a stand for victory, you are on your way to becoming an overcomer.

Deuteronomy 8:2 says, "And you shall remember that the Lord your God led you all the way these forty years in the wilderness, to humble you and test you, to know what was in your heart, whether you would keep his commandments or not."

God didn't bring the tests and trials; God used them to test His people, to know what was in their hearts, and to humble them. The children of Israel came out of Egypt, but they couldn't get Egypt out of their hearts. That is precisely why the apostle Paul said we must forget what is behind and reach for what lies ahead. The tests and trials that come to us can become either stepping-stones or stumbling blocks in our life. They can humble us and show us how much we need the Lord or they can make us prideful. Every stepping-stone is a step in the right direction. I'm not saying you're never going to trip over a stumbling block in your life. You most likely will several times before you can turn those stumbling blocks into stepping-stones. The trick is to get up, shake off the dust, and keep on going. God wants us to grow up so that we can be an asset to His kingdom, mainly so that we won't become stumbling blocks for others, because people are watching us. God was trying to get the children of Israel to put their trust in Him, to see Him as their source.

God promised to give the children of Israel a land flowing with milk and honey, a good land. One day they decided to send men to spy out the Promised Land, to see if it was what God said it was. (Numbers 14) It makes you wonder why they didn't just believe God and take Him at His word. I guess we're not any different from them. One day they chose twelve men

Rosie Rivera

to go spy out the land, and the men found it to be just as God had said. But there was something there they weren't expecting. They weren't counting on giants being there. When God speaks to us and gives us a promise, we never think we are going to encounter giants; we just think God is going to hand everything down to us on a silver platter. We want the promises of God, but we don't want the tests and trials that come with them.

They brought back fruit from the land, proving that it was a good land, but they also brought back a bad report—at least ten of them did. Two of them saw the land as God had promised and said, "We are well able to take the land," but the children of Israel chose to believe the bad report, especially when they heard the ten say they were as grasshoppers in the sight of the giants. God had told them He was going to put out the inhabitants little by little from before them. They didn't have to do anything except believe God. We must believe our God is bigger and mightier than any giant we come in contact with. We can't allow the giants to rob us of our Promised Land. We can't be like the spies and see ourselves as grasshoppers or nobodies. We are children of the King and are as bold as a lions. Our God is able! With Him we are well able to take the land and possess it and overcome the giants.

Many Christians live for today with no plans for the future; they just live one day at a time. God took us out of slavery. We were slaves to sin, and God delivered us out of the power and control of darkness, but many times we remain in bondage because we won't let go of past mistakes or traditions we grew up with. Jesus said the traditions of man make the Word of non-effect. God's Word can't work with traditions; one must be traded for the other.

God planned ahead for you. He planned a race for you to run that would make you more than a conqueror. He wants you to have the victory over temptation and sin. If we want to win in this race, we must follow directions. God's Word is our instruction book. Have you ever attempted to put something together without the instructions because you didn't have time to bother with them? When we do it that way, we often end up with spare parts, and the thing we're putting together doesn't work the way it should.

Shortcuts cannot be taken in this race; taking shortcuts will disqualify you from the prize. Neither can you do it your way. God is not Burger King; we can't have it our way. It must be done God's way.

When you begin running this race, it is wise to know your destination, to have a goal. Everything done in the kingdom of God is done to advance the kingdom of God on this earth. The prize is the high calling of God, eternal life forever. We have to keep reaching even when the going gets tough. One can't run forward while looking back, so it's not wise to keep holding on to one's past. My husband is a great example of this. One day as he was teasing our granddaughter and not looking where he was going, he ran into a pole. It has become a family joke every time our family gets together, but it's a prime example of trying to go forward while looking back.

If we have no vision we have nothing to reach for, nothing to look forward to, nothing to propel us forward, and no reason to run the race.

How many times have you had a dream or a vision of something you would like to do and for one reason or other you gave up on it? Many times we get discouraged because of failures or things that come up that we don't know quite how to handle. Whatever your age is, it's never too late for you to see the fulfillment of your dream.

The apostle Paul said we should run to obtain and not as one beating the air; to do that, we must follow the instruction manual and keep our eye on the goal.

"Do you not know that those who run in a race all run, but one receives the prize? Run in such a way that you may obtain it. And everyone who competes for the prize is temperate in all things. Now they do it to obtain a perishable crown, but we for an imperishable crown. Therefore I run thus: not with uncertainty. Thus I fight: not as one who beats the air. But I discipline my body and bring it into subjection, lest when I have preached to others, I myself should become disqualified" (1 Corinthians 9:24–27 NKJV).

There are volumes of information in these verses. We're all running the same race, so for us there is no competition as there is in an Olympic event. We're not trying to be better than our brother or sister. The purpose of the race is to finish our course. We have different callings with different anointings and different requirements, but all of us are going for the same prize.

Paul encourages us to run to obtain the prize. Don't do it halfheartedly but do it with your whole heart. Put everything you have into it. You must be temperate in all things, and steady, established, grounded in the Word of God, and unmovable. The crown we are waiting to receive is not one that perishes as a gold or silver medal would; it is a crown of life, a crown of righteousness, a victory crown where we hear the Father say, "Well done, thou good and faithful servant." Paul says he does not run with uncertainty. He knows what he wants, and he's going after it with everything he has. And because this prize means so much to him, he disciplines himself so that he will not be disqualified. How much does your race mean to you? Are you willing to discipline yourself so that you will not be disqualified from your race?

Temperance is built through the development of patience. By our nature, that is not one of our strong points. Patience is necessary because God does not work by our time clock. Oh, we'd love it if He did everything by our timing, but most of the time He comes through at the last minute. He's not always on time according to our clocks, but He's never late. Everything in the kingdom of God takes patience. They say Rome wasn't built in a day; neither is the kingdom of God built in a day. If we just do what the Bible says and allow patience to have her perfect work so that we are entire, wanting nothing, we are on our way to bigger and better things.

One of the greatest obstacles you will encounter is going to be other people and their opinions. Why do I say that? Because people say things that can hurt you, they say things that can hinder your race, and many times they won't understand why you want to study the Bible. They might even call you religious, especially if you were recently born again and they haven't been. Sometimes your own family will kind of disown you at first. It's the change they will see in you that's going to make them begin to think there might be something to this after all. It is going to open the door for you to minister the Word of God to them and see them come to the Lord.

The Lord does not desire that any man perish but that all men will come to the knowledge of the truth. We are the ones who carry the good news everywhere we go, beginning with those closest to us. There are going to be many misunderstandings in this race, but we can't allow those misunderstandings to distract us from our goal. We have to keep our eyes on the prize. Keep your eyes focused on Jesus and you will run your race well.

Throughout the Old Testament we read about men and women who ran their race well. The Bible speaks of them in Hebrews 11, which some call the hall of faith because of the great things they did. They were misunderstood many times because what they did didn't always make sense to the human mind.

"But the natural man does not receive the things of the Spirit of God, for they are foolishness unto him; nor can he know them, because they are spiritually discerned" (1 Corinthians 2:14 NKJ).

Take for example Daniel in the lion's den; it didn't even faze him when he was thrown into the lion's den because he knew his God. He just lay down and went to sleep unconcerned about where he was, unconcerned that lions don't take well to humans invading their space. When the king came the next morning to check on him, he was shocked to see Daniel alive.

We see Elijah and the showdown with the prophets of Baal. It made no sense what he did. He wanted to prove who God was. The people had stood between two opinions long enough; it was time for a showdown. Elijah gathered the prophets of Baal and the children of Israel. The prophets were going to prepare an offering for Baal, Elijah was going to prepare one for God, and the god who would answer by fire would be the true God.

The prophets of Baal did as they were told: they prepared the altar and the wood, and the offering upon the altar, and then began crying out to their god. They cried out from morning till noon, but there was no answer. Elijah began teasing them, saying, in effect, maybe your god is on vacation, or busy, or taking a nap. The prophets of Baal began crying out even louder, and cut themselves with knives and lancets until the blood ran everywhere, but there was no answer from their god.

Then it was Elijah's turn. He prepared the altar and the wood, and the sacrifice upon the altar, and had the children of Israel fill four pots with water and pour them out on the burnt sacrifice and the wood. Three times he had them do this, until the water ran all around the altar. Then he called unto the God of Abraham, Isaac, and Israel. As he prayed, fire came down from heaven and consumed the sacrifice and the wood, and licked up the water that was in the trench around the altar. To the natural mind that doesn't happen: water and fire don't mix, not when you want God to answer by fire. Water is used to put out a fire.

You're going to find as you run this race that some things are not going to make sense to you, and that is when you have to trust and believe by faith.

Chapter 6 Questions

1. The _____ will equip you to run your race well.
2. You will encounter many _____ in your race.
3. _____ the Word of God builds stamina, endurance, and spiritual muscle.
4. Running the race takes _____, _____ and _____.
5. The tests and trials of life can become either _____ or _____.
6. Know your _____.
7. Where there is no _____, the people perish.
8. The apostle Paul encourages us to run to _____ _____.
9. Temperance is built through the development of _____.
10. Keep looking unto _____ and you will run your race well.

Chapter 6 suggested Bible readings

Hebrews 12:1–4
Philippians 3:13–14
1 Corinthians 9:27
James 1:1–4

Chapter 6 Answers

1. The Word will equip you to run your race well.
2. You will encounter many obstacles in your race.
3. Exercising the Word of God builds stamina, endurance, and spiritual muscle.
4. Running the race takes discipline, commitment, and humility.
5. The tests and trials of life can become either stepping-stones or stumbling blocks.
6. Know your destination.
7. Where there is no vision, the people perish.
8. The apostle Paul encourages us to run to obtain the prize.
9. Temperance is built through the development of patience.
10. Keep looking unto Jesus and you will run your race well.

Chapter 7

Learning to Walk by Faith

All of our life we walk by faith but don't realize it. The difference between Bible faith and natural faith is that the Bible kind of faith believes what the Word of God says even when we can't see it in the world around us. During the years I have been a Christian, I have learned to trust God. Before coming to the Lord, I trusted in what I could see, feel, taste, smell, or hear. I worried about things I had no control over. I spent many sleepless nights worrying about many things until I understood Proverbs 3:5–6.

Proverbs 3:5–6 NKJV says, "Trust in the Lord with all your heart, and lean not on your own understanding; in all your ways acknowledge Him, and He shall direct your path."

If you want to lean against something, that something must be strong enough to hold you up, and I found that my own understanding was not strong enough to hold me up during the times my faith was being tested. The Word of God is not only a firm foundation on which we stand but is also something we can lean on, knowing it will hold us up in times of trouble. I've learned how to trust in God rather than lean on my own understanding because my own understanding can't be trusted, and to acknowledge His ability to hold me up in every situation. That ability to trust in God and His Word didn't come easy; I had to grow in faith and trust in God and His Word. I could accomplish that only by knowing Him through His Word and a personal relationship with Him.

Everything we do in life must be done by faith. The Bible says the just shall live by faith. It's difficult to live by faith if one does not understand what faith is. We understand natural faith; we get in our car and point it in a certain direction and expect it to get us there without breaking down, getting a flat tire, or running out of gas. Everything we do is done by natural faith. The God kind of faith is much the same as natural faith in that we are putting our faith and confidence in what we can't see and yet we believe it's there.

Hebrews 11:1 NKJV says, "Now faith is the substance of things hoped for, the evidence of things not seen."

The Amplified Bible says, "Now faith is the assurance (confirmation, the title deed) of the things we hope for, being the proof of things [we] do not see and the conviction of their reality [faith perceiving as real fact what is not revealed to the senses]."

Wow! That's great; faith is the assurance, the confirmation, the title deed of things we hope for. Faith is the assurance that God is real. Faith is the assurance that our sins are forgiven. Faith is the title deed; that tells us what we believe is ours because we hold the title deed, and it perceives it as a real fact even though we can't see it with the natural eye or understand it with our understanding. We have to believe by faith that God is who He says He is and that He has done what He says He's done and will do what He says He will do.

"But without faith it is impossible to please and be satisfactory to Him. For whoever would come near to God must [necessarily] believe that God exists and that He is a rewarder of those who earnestly and diligently seek him [out]" (Hebrews 11:6 AB).

We must believe that God is, that God exists, and that God rewards those who diligently seek Him. God is a good God; God looks after His Word to perform it, and His Word does not return unto Him void. To please Him, we must believe even when we can't see it.

We all want to please God, but without faith, it can't be done, because God is a faith God. How can one have faith in a God one cannot see? As we grow in the Word of God, our confidence begins to grow, and we begin to see evidence of what we believe. Our faith begins to increase by the evidence in our life, by the changes we see in ourselves since our conversion, and by everything that exists, even our own existence. If God didn't create us, who did? We didn't pop out of the ground. Where did the ground come from? We didn't evolve, because if we did, we had to evolve out of something, and where did that something come from? It just makes sense to believe that God created us as intelligent beings, with the ability to make choices. I choose to believe that God created me and not that I evolved from an amoeba into a monkey and then an ape and then into me. If that was the case, why are we not seeing our children born that way, and why am I not evolving into something else? This cannot be the ultimate stage of evolution. We believe in God by faith that is backed by evidence we can see all around us. The Bible tells us that we must believe that God rewards those who diligently seek Him. God rewards obedience and faith.

Some denominations teach that God punishes you when you fall short of His expectations and that He uses sickness and disease to teach you. God doesn't need to use the result of sin to teach us; He has given us His Word to teach us. God rewards those who diligently seek Him, those who do it wholeheartedly. God wants you to love Him for who He is and not for what you can get from Him, which is selfish love. God wants us to seek the face of God, not the hand of God. The God kind of love is unconditional and unlimited. God doesn't have love, He is love, and His love is everlasting. There is nothing that can separate you from the love of God.

God is a faith God. He used faith to create the world and everything in it. He created with faith-filled words. He called those things that are not as though they were, and they came into being. God has not lost His creative ability. God is still God.

To the Christian, faith is a lifestyle. The Bible says the just shall live by faith. The Word of God says that you are more than a conqueror; that God always causes you to triumph, that you have the victory through our Lord Jesus Christ. You have to maintain what the Bible says about you through faith by believing God's Word. You must believe it and then act like it's so.

One will never rise above the level of one's faith. If you want great faith, you first have to have faith in God. When you have faith in God, there is nothing impossible to you if you believe. You can begin using your faith to move the mountains in your life.

What kind of mountains are we talking about? We are talking about the things that come against you, the things that hinder you and keep you from obtaining God's best.

God has given you promises in His Word that belong to you, but to obtain them, you sometimes have to fight for what you want. What do I mean by fight? I mean that you have an enemy that wants to defeat you at every turn; he never gives up without a fight. You have to take your faith and stand your ground. The devil wants your faith. Faith is what receives what belongs to you. If the Devil can't keep you ignorant, he will try to steal your faith. The Bible calls him a thief and a liar. He is going to do his best to keep you out of faith. Every time you set out to believe God for something, you are going to have challenges. The more you develop in faith, the less hold the enemy has on you. As you grow in faith knowing that faith works, that you can receive from God, your faith honors God, and your trust and confidence in His Word also increases.

"Fight the good fight of faith, lay hold on eternal life, to the which you were also called, and have confessed the good confession in the presence of many witnesses" (1 Timothy 6:12 NKJV).

Faith is a fight. It can be a good fight or a bad one; it's all going to depend on you. A good fight means you win; a bad fight means you lose. It's always a good fight when you win.

How do I get this kind of faith?

When you were born again, God gave you the measure of faith in seed form. It has to be developed, to grow. Everybody knows that for a seed to grow and produce fruit, it has to be planted in good soil. Every time you speak, you are planting good or bad seed. You're speaking life or death, faith or unbelief.

The Word of God is like a bag of seed that one plants in one's heart. As one meditates on it and puts it into practice, it begins to grow. As you meditate in the Word, it gets down on the inside of you and becomes a reality. When it becomes a reality, then faith comes because the Bible says faith comes by hearing and hearing by the Word of God. You have to do something with the Word of God. You have to put it into practice, and when you do, it begins to work for you. God is not a respecter of persons, but He is a respecter of faith. It is said that faith moves the hand of God. I like to say it this way: faith is the hand that receives from God. Faith begins where the will of God is known. You can't have faith and believe in something if you don't know that it's God's will for you to have it. God's Word is His will.

I see many people living defeated lives because they are still waiting for God to do something while God is waiting for them to move. We work together with God. Every action needs to have a corresponding action. Many Christians are praying, "If it's your will, God." And God is saying, "My Word is my will." When we know the Word of God, we don't have to pray and ask if it's God's will because we know what His Word says. Faith is a very strong spiritual force that produces results when we pray in faith, believing.

We said earlier that faith gives substance to what you believe God for. It is a firm persuasion, an assurance of the existence of something you can't see or feel or perceive with the five senses. Faith is said to be the sixth sense or the sense of the spirit. Faith works somewhat differently than the five senses in that it doesn't go by touch, feeling, sight, smell, or taste. Faith doesn't go by what it feels or sees; faith goes by what it believes, regardless of whether it can be seen or felt. Faith does not consider the circumstances. Faith never sees defeat.

Abraham is called the father of faith. You can begin reading the story of Abraham in Genesis 12. God called Abraham—then called Abram—to leave his kinfolk and go to a land that God would show him. Abram obeyed God and stepped out in faith, not knowing where he was going but trusting God. He and Sarai, his wife, had no children because Sarai was barren; she couldn't have children. Abram and his wife were up in years, yet God told him that He would make him the father of a multitude; God changed his name from Abram to Abraham, which means "father of a multitude." Abraham became a great man of faith, but he didn't get there overnight. He and Sarai had to grow in faith, and in so doing they made mistakes. Thank God the Bible doesn't record only their faith but records their faults as well, letting us know that they were just as human as we are. Abram and Sarai later did what you and I would have done: they tried to help God out.

Maybe they thought God wasn't moving fast enough or that they had to do something to make the promise come to pass. Sarai (later called Sarah) thought maybe God wanted them to have a child through her maid since she herself was unable to bear children. We shouldn't think it strange. After all, they were human just like us, and their reasoning was human reasoning. We have to look deeper into the story to understand the frustration Sarai must have been going through. She was unable to bear a child, and then she was told that her husband would be the father of many nations according to God's Word. It had to be confusing for her. What was her part in all of this? How could it possibly happen, seeing that she was barren? The natural mind couldn't comprehend how this could possibly happen.

Human reasoning forgets that God is almighty and all powerful, and that there's nothing too hard for Him. We don't see Abram resisting or refusing the idea. Maybe he thought it wasn't such a bad idea himself. Sarai gave her maid to her husband and she conceived, but it wasn't the promised child and the problems began. Our world is still experiencing problems today between the descendants of Ishmael and the descendants of Isaac.

Many times we think God is not moving fast enough so we try to help Him out and end up with more problems than we bargained for. When God gives a promise, all that God requires of us is to believe. It's just hard for human beings to understand how great God is and that He doesn't need our help to accomplish what He promised.

We read in the Bible about Abraham's great faith and we think Abraham was always a man of great faith. Abraham had to grow in faith just as we do. God took Abraham for a walk one starry night and showed him all the stars in the sky and how numerous they were. Can you count the stars in the sky? God asked. I'm sure Abraham answered "No, no man can count the stars in the sky." God said, "That's how your descendants are going to be—as numerous as the stars." Abraham began paying more attention to the stars at night, and pretty soon they weren't stars he was seeing anymore. They became faces. He was beginning to catch the vision. God was painting a picture for Abraham, a picture he could grasp and begin to meditate on so that his faith would increase so he could believe in the promised son. Then God took him out on the beach, and as they walked side by side, God drew Abraham's attention to the grains of sand and told him that's how his descendants were going to be.

Abraham was an old man and his wife was past childbearing age, and to make matters worse, she was unable to conceive, but nothing is impossible with God. As Abraham's faith grew, he began to dream of the day when the promised son would arrive through whom many sons would come. Meditating upon God's promise was beginning to change the way Abraham thought.

God and Abraham had a relationship going. They spoke to each other. Abraham became so convinced that he was going to become the father of a multitude; that he no longer doubted what God had promised even when it appeared to be an impossible situation. I'm sure he and Sarah talked about it. Soon Sarah began to catch the vision, too, and to believe it could happen. She received strength to conceive in her old age because she judged God faithful. In the beginning when the angel told Abram that Sarai would conceive and have a child, she laughed, saying, "Me, an old woman, conceive a child when I'm barren?" As her faith grew, so did her confidence in a God who was faithful to His word.

The day came, after God's promise was fulfilled and their son was growing up, that God asked Abraham to offer up his only son as an offering. Abraham didn't disobey God because he had become fully persuaded that if God gave him a son and his descendants were going to come through that son, then God would have to raise him from the dead to fulfill his promise to him about becoming a father of a multitude. At last Abraham's faith had grown to the place where he had no doubt about what God was able to do. Through his relationship with God, he grew to trust Him.

Through faith they received the promise:

> (as it is written, "I have made you a father of many nations") in the presence of Him whom he believed—God, who gives life to the dead and calls those things which do not exist as though they did; who, contrary to hope, in hope believed, so that he became the father of many

nations, according to what was spoken, "so shall your descendants be." And not being weak in faith, he did not consider his own body, already dead (since he was about a hundred years old), and the deadness of Sarah's womb. He did not waver at the promise of God through unbelief, but was strengthened in faith, giving glory to God, and being fully convinced that what He had promised He was also able to perform. (Romans 4:17–20 NKJV)

They didn't receive the manifestation of the promise until twenty-five years later. During that time they were growing stronger in faith. You might not receive the promise of God immediately, but by faith you know it is on its way because God is faithful to His promises. The more time you spend with the Lord in prayer, the more confident you will become in Him. The more you put His Word to work in your life, the more of its manifestation you will see.

Many times while believing for something, you have to hold on to your hope even when there seems to be no hope, when the report says there's no hope; when things seem impossible to the five senses, you need to keep on hoping because hope is the substance of your faith, the evidence that it exists. It's the anchor of your soul. It keeps you focused and steady throughout the waiting period. In time you will become fully persuaded that what God has promised He is able also to perform. Once you become fully persuaded in what you believe, nothing can stop you from believing, and nothing can change your mind.

I have seen God do many miraculous things in my life. I've seen Him turn impossible situations into possibilities. I know what God can do, and I have come to the place where I am fully persuaded that if God said it, He can do it. Yes, my mind gets in the way many times and my thoughts tell me it can't be done, but like I said earlier, I've learned not to trust my thoughts but to trust Him. It's been one of the greatest blessings in my life because with that assurance, peace comes.

When things are going wrong and everything is coming against you, it's easy to doubt and to waver in your faith. We are accustomed to being moved by our five senses. When we begin to doubt, fear comes in, and when fear comes in, faith goes out. If we learn early in our Christian walk to put God's Word first in our life and make it final authority, we will not struggle as much with doubt and unbelief. As long as we are standing in faith, there is no room for doubt.

We must close all doors to the enemy because he wants to steal our faith. Fear comes from Satan; he doesn't want you to succeed. Not that he's concerned about you or your success; he's afraid that you will fulfill the plan of God for your life. He uses different things to distract you from believing. He will try to keep you out of faith by bringing thoughts that preoccupy your mind and things that take up your time. We can't be moved by our emotions; what I mean by that is that many times our emotions get in the way of our faith.

Let's look at the account in the Bible where Jesus comes walking on the water to where His disciples are struggling in the midst of a storm at sea. We want to see how quickly we can go from faith to doubting.

> Now in the fourth watch of the night Jesus went to them, walking on the sea. And when the disciples saw Him walking on the sea, they were troubled, saying, "It is a ghost!" And they cried out in fear. But immediately Jesus spoke to them, saying, "Be of good cheer! It is I; do not be afraid." And Peter answered Him and said, "Lord, if it's you, command me to come to you on the water." So He said, "Come." And when Peter had come down out

of the boat, he walked on the water to go to Jesus.
But when he saw that the wind was boisterous,
he was afraid; and beginning to sink he cried out,
saying, "Lord, save me!" And immediately Jesus
stretched out His hand and caught him, and said
to him, "O you of little faith, why did you doubt?"
(Matthew 14:25–31 NKJV)

Jesus had sent His disciples in a boat to the other side of the
sea, but while they were going, a strong wind that was contrary
to them rose up and the boat was being tossed by the waves.
Jesus went to them walking on the water, and when they saw
Him, they were troubled and cried out in fear because they
thought they were seeing a ghost. When Peter knew it was Jesus,
he said, "If it's you, Lord, command me to come to you on the
water." Jesus said, "Come."

Peter was a man who knew the voice of God even though
sometimes he was too hasty in his actions. It could have been
a ghost. The only way Peter could know whether it was a ghost
or the Lord was through his ability to distinguish the voice of
the Lord. At the word of the Lord, Peter got out of the boat and
began walking to Jesus on the water. He was doing fine, walking
on water, something no other man had ever done, but when he
saw the wind and the waves, he was afraid and began to sink.
Here's what happened. Peter bravely got out of the boat at Jesus'
command, but his mind probably told him, this isn't possible,
man cannot walk on water. He hadn't thought about the strong
wind and the waves that were picking up, but when suddenly
he took his eyes off of Jesus and put them on the circumstances
around him, he began to sink. Jesus asked him, "Why did you
doubt?" He got out of faith.

Many times when we consider the circumstances around
us, we begin to doubt because of what we see and know.
Faith ignores the circumstances. Circumstances will cause you

to take your eyes off the Lord, to waver and to doubt God's ability. Peter was doing fine until he took his eyes off Jesus and began to consider the wind and waves; then he began to waver. Why? Because he was okay with it as long as he was following the Lord's command. Once he got his eyes on the circumstances, fear came in. If he was already walking on the water, what difference was it going to make whether it was windy or the waves were rising? He realized how strong the wind was blowing and saw the waves rising and falling, and thoughts of drowning came into his mind. Frantically he called out to Jesus, "Lord, save me."

We're no different from Peter. We start out strong in faith, strong in the Word, and believing, but that's only as long as everything is going our way. As soon as things begin to take a negative turn, we begin to doubt and cry out to Jesus. Faith doesn't concentrate itself on negative suggestions. Fear and doubt contaminate faith and make it inoperable.

We must be able to recognize faith's enemies. If faith had no enemies, there would be no need to fight, and the Bible says to fight the good fight of faith. Some of faith's enemies are a lack of knowledge of God's Word, a lack of knowledge of who we are in Christ, a lack of knowledge of the authority we have in Christ and a lack of knowledge about the word and what the will of God is for our lives.

If there is no knowledge of what the Word of God says, we will go through life defeated because of a lack of knowledge about His will. If we don't know or understand the authority we have in Christ, we will go through life defeated by the enemy, and if we don't know who we are in Christ, that we are new creatures, that our sins are forgiven, that we are sons of God, we will defeat our own selves by our own lack of self-confidence.

Persistent Faith

What is persistent faith? It's faith that never gives up and never quits. The enemy is always going to try to get you to doubt, to get you out of faith, to get you into fear, and to give up. Doubts are going to come, questions are going to rise up, tests and trials are going to come, and you are going to have to take a strong stand against everything the enemy brings against your faith.

Persistent faith is the kind of faith that continues strong in spite of obstacles; it doesn't take no for an answer and is not moved by circumstances. It always remains strong no matter what it looks like. It overcomes all obstacles. Every time you overcome, every time you jump over obstacles, you become stronger and stronger, and your faith grows by leaps and bounds. It becomes easier to believe and easier to stand firmly without doubting.

In an earlier chapter, we talked about running our race. We can't run in a race unless we have direction. We must run to obtain the prize awaiting us. Each believer should have a goal he or she wants to reach in life and then go after it with everything he or she has. A goal keeps us focused; it strengthens and encourages us as we run this race to the finish line. Hebrews 12:1 says we should run our race with patience. This is where many Christians miss it.

Tests, Trials, and Tribulations Work Patience

Many Christians are praying, *God give me patience,* but they don't recognize that daily we pass up opportunities to grow in patience. Most of us are not patient by nature. We live in a world of fast food, Get N Go's, quick lubes, and instant this and instant that. Many times it carries over into our Christian walk in the sense that we then think we should get instant answers to our prayers, and instant miracles. Patience is something that must be developed, and it is developed through tests, trials, tribulations, and yes, even tears.

I know people who want God to give them patience but don't want the tests and trials that come with developing patience. It's like the children of Israel. They wanted the Promised Land until they saw the giants, and then they quickly changed their minds. God was trying to grow them up. Many people miss the opportunities that are before them because they want to take the route of least resistance; that's the human way. The route of least resistance is hardly ever the best one. Many times in trying to avoid things, we end up getting the very things we tried to avoid. Patience is the ability to keep oneself in check even when one wants to scream or bite someone's head off. Human nature wants to be in control of every situation.

Why is it so hard to be patient, especially when things happen that are beyond our control? It could be that we're putting more trust in what we see than in what we believe. If one never encounters problems in one's life, there is no need for patience, but since we don't live in a dream world, we can be assured that problems are going to come. We should look at every test and trial as an opportunity to develop patience. Patience causes us to mature. When we become mature in the things of God, few negative situations can move us.

Many people think of giving up and quitting every time a problem comes their way. In God's vocabulary there are no words like quit, failure, fear, or defeat, nor should there be in yours. We have to remember that we're not fighting this battle on our own. We have a helper: we have Jesus and the Holy Spirit on the inside and God working with us.

"My brethren, count it all joy when you fall into various trials, knowing that the testing of your faith produces patience. But let patience have its perfect work, that you may be perfect and complete, lacking nothing." (James 1:2–4 NKJV)

Most people find it hard to rejoice when their faith is being tested, yet James says, "Count it all joy when you fall into various trials, knowing that it's going to produce patience." He never said tests and trials are something to be joyful about; he said count it all joy. Why? Because patience is being developed and it's going to benefit you. We have to remember that it's only a test, and the sooner we pass it, the sooner we can move on to bigger and better things.

Two Things Needed for Patience to Be Complete

To be complete means to be perfect or mature, complete and lacking nothing. God is not going to do for us what He has already told us we can do ourselves. He said to let patience have her perfect work. You and I have to be the ones letting patience have her perfect work, but we want God to do the hard part.

God doesn't want His children to be quitters, and He doesn't want them to fail. We should be determined never to accept failure in our Christian walk because the Lord has given us everything we need to succeed at everything we endeavor to do.

You must learn to go through those trying times with patience, knowing that He never leaves you or forsakes you, and knowing that you will never face anything in life that you and God cannot handle. Patience endures when things get hard. God wants us to develop patience because it is one of the fruits of the spirit and one thing that produces character in us. If you ever want to accomplish anything in life, it's going to take dedication, commitment, and discipline.

Character Builders

What are character builders? Character builders are the things that build character in you. Personality will take you places, but character will keep you there. Character is what defines who you are and what you believe. Character is what God is looking for in His children because it shows growth. When God is looking to promote someone, He looks at his or her character.

The apostle Paul was a patient man. They would beat him, stone him, and leave him for dead, and he'd get right back up again and go back to the very people who stoned him and left him for dead. He learned how to be content in whatever situation he found himself in. Many problems would be solved today if we only learned to be content in whatever situation we find ourselves in.

One time it looked like they weren't going to make it because of the storm that rose up at sea. Everybody was acting out of fear and despair, but Paul was calm and collected. When he and his traveling companion were beaten and thrown into jail, he didn't panic; at midnight he and Silas began praying and singing praises unto God, and God began to work on their behalf. Patience teaches one to be content in whatever situation one finds oneself in, whether waiting in line at the grocery store, driving down the freeway in a city, or waiting in a restaurant to be served. Patience teaches us to be content when things are not going our way because we know our God always causes us to triumph, and He delivers us out of all our tribulations. God has made you more than a conqueror, the head and not the tail, above only and not beneath. You are blessed when you come in and when you go out.

Maybe the things you're going through at the moment are not making you jump for joy and you don't feel like singing and praising God. You feel that way at the moment, but later, when the thing you're waiting for comes to pass, when the things that used to bug you don't bug you anymore, when you are able to tolerate what you couldn't tolerate, you'll know your patience is being developed.

Christians should be different from the rest of the world. We live in a very impatient world because of selfishness. If you don't believe it, just stand in a grocery line and see what happens when someone at the front of the line is writing a check, or an item doesn't have the price on it and you are on your lunch break and have to get back to work.

Most of us don't like waiting, much less waiting patiently. It takes patience to achieve the result we desire to see. The Bible tells us that when we wait upon the Lord, our strength is renewed. It's a simple little exercise that produces much. A person who lifts weights knows that strength has to be developed just as patience does. How does one increase one's strength? Strength increases as the weight is increased. Our definition of wait and God's definition of wait are two different things. To God one day is as a thousand years and a thousand years are as one day. Waiting is required for one's patience to develop.

Why discuss patience when studying faith? The Bible says it's through faith and patience that we inherit the promise. Faith is what gives substance to what we hope for, even though we can't see it. Through faith we have the assurance that it exists, and so we patiently wait for it to come to pass.

Chapter 7 Questions

1. The Bible says the just shall live by _____.
2. Without faith it is _____ to please God.
3. Faith _____.
4. God rewards those who _____ seek him.
5. To the Christian, faith is a _____.
6. You will never rise above the _____ of your faith.
7. _____ the good fight of faith.
8. Faith comes by _____ and _____ by the Word of God.
9. To receive from God you must become fully _____ that what God has promised He is able also to perform.
10. Faith ignores the _____.

Chapter 7 suggested Bible readings

Romans 1:17
Hebrews 11:6
1Timothy 6:12
Romans 4:21

Chapter 7 Answers

1. The Bible says the just shall live by faith.
2. Without faith it is impossible to please God.
3. Faith believes.
4. God rewards those who diligently seek him.
5. To the Christian faith is a lifestyle.
6. You will never rise above the level of your faith.
7. Fight the good fight of faith.
8. Faith comes by hearing and hearing by the Word of God.
9. To receive from God you must become fully persuaded that what God has promised He is able also to perform.
10. Faith ignores the circumstances.

Chapter 8

What Is Righteousness?

When we understand righteousness and understand that we have been made the righteousness of God in Christ Jesus according to 1 Corinthians 5:21 ("For He made him who knew no sin to be sin for us, that we might become the righteousness of God in Him"), we will stop struggling with sin and temptation. We have been made the righteousness of God, not through religion, not by the law, not by works but through the sacrifice of our Lord and Savior Jesus Christ.

The law made no man perfect because the law required sacrifices that could never remove sin. The High Priest went into the holy place once a year with the blood of bulls and goats that could never take away sin. It couldn't purge their conscience of dead works. Year after year they were reminded of their sinfulness. The only offering that was pleasing to God was the sacrifice of His Son. The blood of Jesus was the only blood that could take away sin and purge our conscience from dead works so that we could serve Him without fear and trembling.

We can't approach God through our good works; we can't work hard enough to gain righteousness. Righteousness is a gift given to every believer. None of us were good enough to merit God's righteousness. If you're given a gift, that gift has to be received for it to benefit you. In the same way righteousness must be received by faith. You don't need to feel righteous before you can receive the gift.

"For if by one man's offense death reigned through the one, much more those who receive abundance of grace and of the gift of righteousness will reign in life through the One, Jesus Christ" (Romans 5:17 NKJV).

Through the gift of righteousness you can reign over sin and temptation in your life. Sin and temptation no longer lord it over you. You begin to reign in life over everything that comes your way. Sin no longer is in control of your life; you are. Things began to change in your life. You'll find you are in control of your thoughts and how you handle difficult situations. You are no longer conscious of sin and condemnation.

The mind is the battleground. In the mind, one wins or loses. The mind is like the canvas of a painter. Everything one sees, hears, and speaks paints pictures in the mind, and one responds accordingly, whether good or bad. We have to let the Word of God paint the pictures in our mind. It's the Word of God and how we see ourselves in the Word that begins to change the way we think and act. The Bible tells us that looking into the Word is like looking into a mirror. When we look into the mirror, we see our defects and what needs to be changed. So it is when looking into the Word of God. It shows us where we need to make changes and tells us how to do it.

Righteousness is God's way of being right or doing things God's way.

Righteousness is what God imparted to you when you came into the family of God. You were not in right standing with God because of sins separation. God clothed you in His righteousness the day you accepted Him as your Lord and Savior. It wasn't by any good works that you did, or anything religious; it was an act of God.

Now that we've learned some things about faith, it's time to learn about righteousness. Webster's dictionary and Rogets Thesaurus 2004, defines righteousness as, "godliness, holiness, and sanctity." When we were born again, we became reunited with God. Godliness, holiness, and sanctity—all characteristics of God—were placed in our spirit, which received the new life of God, but like we saw earlier, it was our spirit that received new life; we still have the flesh and the soul to work with. As we grow in Christ, these characteristics should be growing in us and coming forth on the outside.

Righteousness gives us right standing with God. We are no longer separated from Him. Righteousness is God's way of doing things. When righteousness is understood, the battle with sin, temptation, and guilt is over. Righteousness frees one from guilt and condemnation. The enemy of your faith doesn't want you to feel good about yourself, especially when you are weak in your faith and fail. He wants you to feel guilty and full of condemnation. He knows that when one understands righteousness, it makes one bold. Righteousness makes us run to God not away from Him. We gain confidence through our right standing with God. It gives one confidence to come boldly before the throne of grace.

Righteousness gives us the ability to resist the temptation to feel guilty, to feel regret for past failures and shortcomings, and to feel insecure about who we are. Jesus came to help us be pleasing to God. He knows our human nature and knows we're going to miss it sometimes, but it's not a reason to feel condemnation.

"But seek first the kingdom of God and His righteousness, and all these other things shall be added unto you" (Matthew 6:33).

Everything we need for life and godliness will be added unto us if we seek first the kingdom of God and His righteousness. If the kingdom of God and His righteousness are first, things it behooves us to have an understanding of what the kingdom of God is and what righteousness is. We have studied in previous chapters that the work Jesus came to earth to do was accomplished and that it's a finished work; nothing has to be added to it. He did it for us so that we could live the abundant life He died to give us. It's not based on anything we do or how good we are, but on a finished work. Righteousness is not based on what we can do. It must be received by faith in believing what the Bible says.

"And He said unto them, to you it has been given to know the mystery of the kingdom of God; but to those on the outside, all things come in parables" (Mark 4:11 NKJV).

When you are serious about learning about the kingdom of God, the things spoken in parables will become clear to you. Once a parable is revealed to you, you have the obligation to walk in it. In God's kingdom there is no sickness or disease, there is no failure, and it makes no difference what side of the tracks you were born on. All humans were born on the wrong side of the tracks; all were born sinners in need of a savior. Some people use that as an excuse for the way they are, by saying, "I'm this way because I came from a dysfunctional family." We all came from dysfunctional families, no matter how intelligent we were; we were all lost, and we were all separated from the life of God. In our society today it is much easier to blame someone else for one's problems than to take responsibility for one's own actions. A man blames his wife, a child blames his parents, an employee blames his boss; even Adam said, "It's the woman you gave me." The blame game is not anything new.

The Bible says there are none righteous because we were all born into this world with the sin nature. None of us was born pure and holy and sanctified. So what is righteousness, and how do I get it?

Can I get righteous by doing good deeds, by being religious, by not drinking, smoking, cursing, or eating certain kinds of foods?

The Israelites sought after righteousness and never attained it. Why? They didn't know what they were looking for. They thought righteousness came by keeping the law, by following strict rules and regulations. They didn't understand God's righteousness. The Bible says they had a zeal for God, but it was zeal based on the laws and traditions of man. The apostle Paul said they had a zeal for God, but it wasn't according to knowledge. That's why we are studying righteousness, so we can have a right understanding of what we're looking for and how to attain it. The Israelites were trying to earn righteousness by keeping the law. They misunderstood the purpose of the law. The law was given so that they would know what sin was; before the law, there was no knowledge of sin.

God gave the law for them to live by. God, knowing that man could not become righteous by works, provided a system so that the sins of the people could be covered temporarily until Jesus came.

People misunderstood the law; thus the law became a heavy yoke of bondage, a bondage they couldn't get rid of, made up of rules and regulations they couldn't keep. That bondage became a ball and chain they carried around with them daily, while they tried to do something to become righteous. They kept struggling to meet the demands of the law, and in so doing, they got further and further away from God, so that when their deliverer came, they didn't even recognize Him. The Pharisees tried to convert people to their religion. It wasn't so much about God anymore; their religion became their god.

There's a misunderstanding in the church today, with many still believing they have to do good works to obtain righteousness. In many of our churches today, people become preoccupied with religion and religious acts, trying to be good enough to be accepted by God to the point that their works become their religion. Many religions today try to convert people to their religion rather than to Jesus Christ. Christians don't have religion; they have relationship.

Jesus and the reason He came to earth is the whole theme of the Bible. If it had not been for His sacrifice, none of us would be saved. Jesus said, "Go into the entire world and make disciples, teaching them to observe and to do all that I have commanded." He didn't tell us to go into all the world and make converts of the law or the traditions of man.

In studying righteousness we're going to find that God is not pleased when our works become our religion and we forget what Jesus has done for us. God is not pleased when we go about trying to establish our own righteousness by what we can do using our own strength and ability.

Adam and Eve were created in the image of God. They were righteous because they had the nature of God in them. They could approach God without feelings of shame and guilt. God would come down in the cool of the evening and visit with them. Sin and unrighteousness came in when Adam and Eve disobeyed God and were separated from the life of God. God had to expel them from the garden so that they would not eat of the Tree of Life and live forever in a sinful state. Since that time, man has tried to work his way back to God in his own way rather than God's way.

Jesus Christ is the door to righteousness, and all we have to do is believe with our heart and confess with our mouth that Jesus is the Son of God whom God raised from the dead. It's so simple, yet many people miss it because they try to make it complicated.

How does righteousness come?

"That if you confess with your mouth the Lord Jesus and believe in your heart that God has raised Him from the dead, you will be saved. For with the heart one believes unto righteousness, and with the mouth confession is made unto salvation" (Romans 10:9–10 NKJV).

Man believes with the heart unto righteousness. Righteousness is a gift freely given to us by God; all we have to do is receive it. The Bible says in Romans 5:17 that if we receive the abundance of grace and the gift of righteousness, we can reign in life by

Jesus Christ, not in our own righteousness but in His. Once we receive the gift, Gods begins to show us how to walk in righteousness.

The apostle Paul wrote in Romans 7 about the struggle he had between the spirit and the flesh, trying not to sin, trying to be good enough but always ending up doing the very things he didn't want to do. In our own strength, we can never live a sinless life. In ourselves, we can't be good enough. In ourselves, we are going to make mistakes and miss the mark. But we're not doing things in ourselves when we depend upon God's righteousness. Through the Word of God and understanding of God's righteousness, you can become stronger in the spirit and overcome the desires of the flesh. Jesus Christ is the only one who can deliver you from a life of dead works.

You have been made the righteousness of God in Christ. Your righteousness is based on what Jesus did and not on anything you have done. Righteousness gives you the right to stand before God without a sense of guilt, inferiority, or condemnation. You can approach God as if you never sinned because He is seeing you through the blood of His Son Jesus. You don't have to be afraid of God.

Many people, because they don't understand righteousness, go back into sin when they miss it because instead of running to God, they run from Him, feeling unworthy and condemned. Satan knows if he can keep you away from God, he has you where he wants you, so he uses condemnation to entrap you. The Bible tells us that when we go to God and confess our sin, He is faithful and just to forgive us our sin and to cleanse us from all unrighteousness. (1John 1:9) That means He will put you right back into right standing with Himself. Your righteousness is not based on what you've done but on what He's done for you.

The Bible tells us that now we can come boldly to the throne room of grace to obtain help and grace in a time of need. Why?

Jesus our high priest has gone in before us and purchased our salvation. His sacrifice not only covers sin, but erases it. His blood has purged our conscience from dead works to serve the living God. When our conscience is purged, there is no more consciousness of sin, no more remembrance of sin; we can come before Him as if we'd never sinned.

God was grieved with the children of Israel because they did not know His ways. They tried to get to God their own way, so God said, "They shall not enter my rest." (Hebrews 4:3) God warns us in His Word so that we do not grieve God in the same way as they did. The Bible teaches us to exhort one another daily so that our hearts will not be hardened through the deceitfulness of sin.

How can we become hardened by the deceitfulness of sin? We can harden our heart when we sin and miss the mark and do not go to God in repentance. The enemy will come, bringing condemnation, and little by little he'll begin to draw you away from God. He will tell you, "You've failed God, He doesn't love you anymore. Why try? It's not going to make any difference now." What you do at that point does make a difference. You must put your confidence in what God says and not in what the enemy says. Your confidence and your trust should always be in the Word of God and in God's faithfulness to forgive you and to cleanse you from all unrighteousness. You have to become confident in His righteousness. You now have free access to God. You can go to Him boldly and without fear. You have been justified by grace. God sees you just as if you never sinned. You are the righteousness of God in Christ Jesus.

Seek first the kingdom of God and His righteousness, and all these other things shall be added unto you. Don't seek after things. Seek after God and His righteousness. God never takes away from you. He always adds and multiplies. God is a good God who loves to bless His children when they obey Him.

Works of Righteousness

"What? I thought you said works can't make you righteous." That's true, but I'm not talking about doing works to obtain righteousness; I'm talking about works that righteousness produces. If you are the righteous of God—and you are if you are born again—then righteousness causes you to produce works that are pleasing to God.

We've already discussed how the enemy wants to control you through your thought life. That's how he was able to deceive Eve by making suggestions that she fell for. The Bible tells us that we are to be transformed by the renewing of our mind. As we learn to control the thoughts that come to our mind, we are able to restrain ourselves from doing or saying things that are displeasing to God.

The mind is the battleground where battles are either won or lost. There's always a battle going on in your mind. You are your worst enemy. You can talk yourself out of anything. If you think you can't, you can't. The mind is a powerful thing. Satan wants to inject thoughts of defeat and failure and doubt so that you become intimidated and believe his lies. God wants you to be strong in the spirit of your mind, to be in control of your thoughts. God wants you free from strongholds that hold you captive.

"For though we walk in the flesh, we do not war according to the flesh." For the weapons of our warfare are not carnal but mighty in God for pulling down strongholds, casting down arguments and every high thing that exalts itself against the knowledge of God, bringing every thought into captivity to the obedience of Christ, and being ready to punish all disobedience when your obedience is fulfilled" (2 Corinthians 10:3–6 NKJV)

We walk in the flesh because we are flesh beings, and when the Bible uses the word carnal, it's talking about the desires of the flesh. Now that you are born again, you no longer respond according to the flesh because now the weapons of your warfare are no longer carnal weapons.

We are not supposed to entertain bad thoughts because those thoughts are converted into imaginations, which develop into strongholds. The converted human mind becomes a sorting ground where thoughts are being either received or rejected. Satan is good at using the power of suggestion to lure God's people into captivity. We saw how he lured Eve into sin in the Garden of Eden.

We mentioned before how thoughts paint pictures in the mind. The human mind is a powerful thing. The Christian's mind is meant to be the canvas where God paints pictures of good things through meditation of His Word. God paints pictures on the canvas of one's mind through thought. The enemy also uses thoughts to paint negative pictures because he knows the power of thought.

The Bible says you are to be transformed by the renewing of your mind. It's not up to God; it's up to you. Why does the Bible say you are to be renewed in the spirit of your mind? We were conformed to this world and we thought according to the ways of the world: Our thought was if it feels good, do it or whatever will be, will be."

Many Christians come into the kingdom of God with thoughts of failure and thinking they can never amount to anything. They think they have to live in poverty, or that they have to be sick. They think that is their lot in life and they are supposed to just accept it. Jesus came showing us a different way because He is the way, the truth, and the life. He said He came that we might have life, and that we might have it more abundantly.

Sin was a way of life; man didn't know there was any other way because of the sin nature that was in him. Now that we are new creatures in Christ, we are not to be conformed anymore to this world but are to be transformed by renewing our mind to God's ways.

The Bible says we are not our own, that we were bought with a price, so then what we allow affects not only us but God also. It affects our relationship with the Lord. It affects what God can do through us, and it affects the anointing God placed in us to minister to the needs of others. Since you belong to God, it stands to reason that He wants your eyes, your ears, your mouth, your body, and your soul and spirit. He wants all of you, not just your spirit.

Understanding righteousness gives one the ability to live a life in right standing with God and to gain the victory over sin. When we sin, the Bible tells us to repent, receive our forgiveness, and go on as if we had never sinned. Because we have believed in the Lord Jesus, we know that we have been approved by God and accepted by Him.

God was in Christ reconciling the world unto Himself. Remember in the beginning of this book, we talked about how man became separated from God through his disobedience. Jesus Christ was the only one who could repair the damage caused by the fall. God was in Christ reconciling the world because the world was separated from God through sin. God through His righteousness brought us back into right standing with Him. Now we can stand before Him with no shame or feelings of unworthiness.

You're not always going to do things right; you are going to make mistakes and miss the mark s ometimes, but you can do your best to live a life that pleases God.

We must train ourselves to listen to our heart. Every time we go against the conviction of our heart, we end up doing wrong. We can't ignore the voice of our conscience. We now have the spirit of God living in us, and that makes our heart a safe guide to follow.

Chapter 8 Questions

1. What is righteousness?
2. Righteousness is a _____.
3. How do I become righteous?
4. Righteousness frees one from _____ and _____.
5. Seek _____ the kingdom of God and His _____.
6. The Bible says none are _____.
7. Righteousness does not come by _____ or by the _____.
8. The law had _____ and _____ man could not keep.
9. If we're not careful, works can become our _____ _____ .
10. God seeks _____, not _____.

Chapter 8 suggested Bible reading

Romans 5:17
2 Corinthians 5:21
Matthew 6:33
Romans 3:10
Romans 4:13–16

Chapter 8 Answers

1. Righteousness is God's way of doing things.
2. Righteousness is a gift
3. One becomes righteous through Jesus Christ.
4. Righteousness frees one from guilt and condemnation.
5. Seek first the kingdom of God and His righteousness.
6. The Bible says none are righteous.
7. Righteousness does not come by works or by the law.
8. The law had rules and regulations man could not keep.
9. If we're not careful, works can become our religion.
10. God seeks relationship, not religion.

Chapter 9

Depending upon God's Grace

Why do we need to learn to depend upon God's grace? When we learn to depend upon God's grace, we cease from doing our own works. We cease trying to please God through religion and the law. We cease trying to please God through our own righteousness.

There has been much controversy about grace. Some have taken the concept of grace overboard and are teaching that it's okay to live in sin because the price for sin has been paid; therefore, they say, we are forgiven, for the past, present, and future. That erroneous teaching has caused many people to go back into their old lifestyle. I know ministries that are no longer in operation because they got off on the teaching that it's okay to sin because sin's been paid for. It has caused much confusion among Christians who knew those people's ministry before they went astray. That kind of teaching is causing much confusion in the body of Christ. That erroneous teaching has ruined many ministries and marriages. The Bible teaches that we are to take off the old man and put on the new, which is created in true righteousness and holiness. A Christian does not practice sin.

Every time a "new" teaching comes around, I do what I was taught in Bible school: I don't jump on the bandwagon right away but weigh what is being said in the light of God's Word. It's true that the Bible says that when Jesus made an end of sacrifice for sin, He sat down at the right hand of the Father and now our sins are forever forgiven, but that doesn't give us a license to live in sin. It is clear in the Bible that God wants us to live a changed life, and to do it, we must depend upon His grace.

What is grace?

GRACE: God's Righteousness at Christ's Expense

It is God's ability working in you to do the things you cannot do using your own human strength. Man by nature is weak without God. A sincere relationship with God is the only thing that is able to keep one from a life of sin. Grace is God's influence in your life, and in turn, your lifestyle becomes a reflection of that influence. When one sees folks acting like the Devil, there's no question about whose influence they have come under.

The Bible says that where sin abounds, grace does much more abound, meaning that grace is a much more powerful force than sin. Grace is what keeps us walking upright and keeps us in line. Many times the truths in God's Word are taken out of context and made to say what the reader wants to hear. One doesn't need more grace to keep one in sin; sinning was done without grace. We need grace in our lives to keep us from the deceitfulness of sin. Sin is deceitful. It will entice you to sin and then condemn you. Yes, the Bible says there is pleasure in sin for a season, but it also says that when sin is finished, it brings forth death. It appears to be pleasurable at first and last for a season, but that season always comes to an end.

Different Kinds of Grace

Saving Grace

"For all have sinned and fall short of the glory of God, being justified freely by His grace through the redemption that is in

Christ Jesus, whom God set forth as a propitiation by His blood, through faith, to demonstrate His righteousness because in His forbearance God had passed over the sins that were previously committed, to demonstrate at the present time His righteousness, that He might be just and the justifier of the one who has faith in Jesus" (Romans 3:23–26 NKJV).

We have been freely justified by grace, just as if we had never sinned. God not only saved us from the influence of sin in our life, but is constantly saving us from ourselves. Many times we are our own worst enemy. Thank God that He overlooks our sins and offers us the free gift of His grace. The gift is free, but it didn't come cheap. Thank God He made provision for our sin from the foundation of the world because we could never be good enough to earn God's grace.

Grace is a gift from God to us. It is unmerited favor, getting what we didn't deserve. We didn't deserve God's salvation. We didn't deserve to be forgiven. We didn't even deserve to be made the righteousness of God in Christ. God in His love and His mercy made us new creatures in Christ and erased all of our sins, nailing them to His cross. He has given us eternal life. Mercy is not getting what you deserve. We deserved to be punished for our sins and to suffer the penalty for them. We deserved to go to hell. God is a merciful God. He chose to forgive us and put us back in right standing with Himself. He has given us another chance to start over.

Grace, God's Power to Reign in Life

"For if by one man's offense death reigned through the one, much more those who receive abundance of grace and of the gift of righteousness will reign in life through the one Jesus Christ" (Romans 5:17 NKJV).

In order to reign in life, one must be able to recognize one's weaknesses and inabilities. It's always easy to see someone else's weaknesses, to see the splinter in our brother's eye, but it's not as easy to recognize the beam in our own eye. As human beings, we tend to judge people by their actions.

I once heard a preacher say that after a meeting, he was going to his hotel room, and as he was getting into the elevator, he saw a drunken man being carried by two other men. He said he looked at the man and thought, how disgusting, and at that moment, the Holy Spirit spoke up in him and said, "The only difference between him and you is Jesus Christ." Immediately he repented of his thoughts. I haven't forgotten that statement; it has had an effect on my life. The only difference between me and the sinner is Jesus Christ.

We like to use our weaknesses as excuses for the things we do. We must do something about our weaknesses or they will always be a stumbling block. Using our weaknesses as excuses for the things we do keeps us from facing reality and doing something about it. That is why we need God's grace to help us overcome our weaknesses. For us to be free, we first must acknowledge our weaknesses. Once we acknowledge our weaknesses, we can begin working to turn them into strengths. First there must be in us that desire to change. Recognizing our weaknesses doesn't make us weak but humbles us so that God can lift us up by His grace.

Humility is not a weakness; rather, it's a strength that puts you over the top. It's recognizing your need for God's grace, recognizing that the power flows through you, not from you. Many times we have to come to the end of ourselves before we are able to recognize how God's grace is working in our lives. They say hindsight is better than foresight.

Maybe the very things you are going through now are the very things God wants to use to develop the leader in you. You're not in this battle by yourself. You have someone you can depend on and someone you can put your confidence in. As long as you are able to handle things on your own, there is no need for His grace. We need God's grace when we come to the end of ourselves and don't know what to do. God wants us to recognize our dependence upon Him.

God has graced every one of us. What gift or talent has God graced you with? When you find where your grace is, it will be a plus for you because you will always function best in the area where you are graced. That is when your gift will make room for you. You won't have to struggle trying to make room for it. If you are gifted in a certain area, everyone will recognize it as a gift from God. God wants your talents to be used for His glory, but you must surrender those talents to Him so that His anointing can flow through you.

There are two things every Christians should recognize:

Recognize what you cannot do yourself. That will take the struggle out of life and will keep you from being frustrated. Then recognize and accept what God can do through you. Know who you are in Christ. You are not an old sinner saved by grace. You were an old sinner, but grace saved you, and now you are a new creature in Christ. You are the righteousness of God in Christ, accepted by Him. You are an heir and joint heir with Jesus Christ. You are victorious because your victory is in Christ.

Serving Grace

Serving grace is God's ability working in you to help you serve in the area God has called you to. It doesn't work only for ministers; it also works for the helps ministry. What would ministers do if there was no ministry of helps? Ministry is not a one-man show. There are no Lone Rangers in God's kingdom. We are all joined together by that which each joint supplies. I mentioned before that it's all about people. Jesus came to serve, not to be served. We should be just as willing to serve others and help them grow in grace.

God gives people grace to stand in the office He calls them to. For some it may be a pulpit ministry, for others it may be teaching children, and for others it may be serving others. Life is all about serving. You cannot be satisfied in life until you are serving someone in one capacity or other. Why is this? As you grow in the Word, you also grow closer to people because that is where God's heart is.

The Bible says whatever your hand finds to do, do it, and do it as unto the Lord. That simply means doing everything we do without grumbling and complaining. We don't begrudge serving when we do it as unto the Lord. All promotion comes from God. Whatever we do for the Lord never goes unnoticed. When it's done as unto the Lord, there is no room for grumbling and complaining. It's important not only what you do but how you do it.

God equips us for service, and with that, he gives us the ability to overlook a lot of things. People aren't always going to appreciate you or the things you do for them. We learn through the grace of God to be kind to everyone regardless of whether we're appreciated or not because our rewards come from the Lord and not from man.

Standing Grace

Standing grace is the ability to stand no matter what comes your way. Standing grace will keep you going when others quit and give up. All of us are going to face difficult times at one time or another; the outcome of those difficult times is going to depend on your ability to stand. God gives us that ability when we need it. Standing grace is the power of God released and working in an individual, making him able to reign.

"But may the God of all grace, who called us to His eternal glory by Christ Jesus, after you have suffered awhile, perfect, establish, strengthen, and settle you" (1 Peter 5:10).

God wants for us to mature. He doesn't want us to be tossed to and fro with every wind of doctrine that comes our way. He wants us to be established so that we're not so easily moved. He wants us settled in our faith and in our trust in Him.

God's grace is so wonderful that it empowers you to overcome the difficulties that come your way. It gives you the strength to stand even when it seems that you can't stand any longer. The pressure seems to be increasing instead of decreasing, the problems seem to grow bigger overnight, and you feel like the kitten on the poster hanging on to the branch for dear life with the words underneath that say, "Hang in there." God gives you the ability to hang in there, to stand when you feel like you can't stand any more, to hang in there when you feel like it's taking everything you have just to hang on. When I went to Bible school, we were told, "If you are willing to stand as long as you have to, you won't be standing long. God will come through for you because He is a faithful God." I have found it to be true in my life.

Many Christians fail because if an answer doesn't come immediately, they give up. The answer isn't always going to come tomorrow, but if you keep standing and trusting, it will come in God's timing. Everything doesn't get handed down to us on a silver platter; many times we have to fight for what we want, and many times we are going to be standing a long time. Payday doesn't always come on Saturday, but it always comes on time.

The apostle Paul said to fight the good fight of faith. We must remember that we do not fight against flesh and blood. Our foes are unseen by the naked eye. We fight with spiritual weapons. The most powerful weapon we have is the Word of God. When Jesus was being tempted by the Devil in the wilderness, Jesus said it is written, and the Devil was not able to stand against Him. Faith is another spiritual weapon because faith says; I believe even if I can't see it, therefore I will stand until I see the desired result.

I have seen God's grace work in my life time and time again. Yes, there have been times when I wanted to quit, give up, and let go, but grace kept me standing, holding on when I didn't think I could hold on anymore. I look back now and can see the hand of grace at work in every situation. In the most difficult times of my life, God's grace has sustained me. I thank God for the wonderful grace He has bestowed upon us. I have had my share of hard blows in my life, but I can testify that the Lord has delivered me out of them all.

Grace is not a license to sin; grace is the strength that keeps us from sinning. The apostle Paul said, in Romans 6:1–2, "What shall we say then? Shall we continue in sin that grace may abound? God forbid. How shall we, that are dead to sin, live any longer therein?"

"Moreover, the law entered that the offence might abound, but where sin abounded, grace did much more abound" (Romans 5:20).

There are erroneous teachings out there that say that because we now live under grace, it's okay to sin; we are living in the grace period, and there is no condemnation to those who are in Christ Jesus. It's true that the Bible says there is no condemnation to those who are in Christ, but it also says, "who walk after the spirit and not after the flesh." We are living in the last days, and the Bible says there will be scoffers in the last days and that those who have itching ears will seek out preachers who will tickle their ears with what they want to hear.

God's grace is greater than sin. Where sin abounds, grace abounds much more. In other words, grace gives us the ability to resist sin. When we were under the law, we had no ability to resist sin, but now that Jesus has paid the price for our sins, He has given us the power to overcome it in our life. Actually, the Bible says that if we receive the abundance of grace and the gift of righteousness, we shall reign in life by one, Jesus Christ. Grace gives us the ability to reign over the circumstances in our lives. That grace God has given us reigns through righteousness. Righteousness is God's way of doing things. If we do things God's way, we can't fail. If our lifestyle is right and our character is molded after the Word, then grace is obligated to come in and strengthen us and give us the ability to stand against all the evil that comes against us and to reign in this life with Christ.

Christians have trouble seeing grace work for them because they are too conscious of natural things—of their surroundings and their circumstances. God is greater than their circumstances. When we put our trust in the great God whom we serve, there is nothing too big that God cannot change by grace. Our problem is that we are trying too hard to fix our circumstances without relying on the grace of God.

When the apostle Paul found himself in a place he could not get out of on his own, he begged God to take away his problem, but God said, "My grace is sufficient for you." Why wouldn't God just take away his problem? It's obvious that it was a constant thorn in his side that refused to let up. God wants us to rely on His grace because when we are weakest, that's when it goes to work for us. Paul got a revelation of grace. Then he was able to rejoice when tests, trials, and tribulations came his way because that's when God's grace came into his life to make him an overcomer, to cause him to reign over the circumstances instead of being overtaken by them. If every Christian would learn to rely on God's grace, they would have a much more victorious life than they have.

Grace has done so much for us. By grace you have been saved through faith, and that not of yourselves: it is a gift of God, not of works, lest anyone should boast. (Ephesians 2:8-9 NKJV) Grace is a gift. It cannot be obtained by works. We can't obtain grace by our good works; we obtain good works by grace.

Grace and righteousness go hand in hand. You can't have one without the other. God has made us righteous by the death and resurrection of His Son. He did all the work. Now it's up to us to take the gift He offers freely.

The Bible says to grow in grace. How does one grow in grace?

The number one way to grow in grace is to study the Word of God. It's God's Word that is going to change you, the way you think, the way you speak, and the way you act. God's Word is alive and full of power, ready to change your life. Looking into the Word is where you are going to see yourself as God sees you and you will be changed from glory to glory into His image.

Growing in grace requires humbling of one's self.

James 4:6 says, "God resists the proud but gives grace to the humble."

A prideful person says, "I don't need help, I can do it myself." A prideful person does things his own way and doesn't want to be told how things should be done. A prideful person cannot admit failure. He believes he is always right. A humble person, on the other hand, admits he can't do it on his own. God can work with a humble person. God exalts a humble person and takes him to heights he's never known.

Growing in grace requires prayer.

Prayer is to a Christian what a lifeline is to a drowning man. There is power in prayer. You will never meet a powerful Christian who doesn't have a prayer life. Praying people are powerful people. God knows those who pray. Those who pray know God. But guess what: the Devil knows a praying Christian.

Prayer produces strong, steadfast Christians. Praying Christians exercise authority on the earth. The Bible tells us to come boldly to the throne of grace to obtain mercy and find grace in a time of need. A praying Christian knows he can go boldly to the throne of God and obtain what he needs. He has confidence in God and his Word.

God's grace can never be exhausted, and His mercy is new every morning. A Christian who prays doesn't struggle with the things a non-praying person struggles with. Prayer produces grace, and grace produces peace and rest from one's own works. When we put our trust in God, we don't have to struggle with problems using our own strength. God gives us the strength to conquer every trial that comes our way.

Prayer keeps one in the grace of God, which keeps one from fainting when the going gets tough. Jesus tried to get His disciples to pray with Him when He was going through agony in the garden of Gethsemane before He was arrested, but they slept instead. If Peter had prayed, he would have been strong enough to resist the urge to deny the Lord. Jesus said, "The spirit is willing, but the flesh is weak." Strength comes from prayer.

Grace comes through prayer. Grace changes you so that you can use your faith to change things. The areas you were weak in before prayer are now strengthened so that grace works for you.

John called Jesus the Lamb of God who takes away the sin of the world. He also said Jesus was full of grace and truth. We need to have a personal relationship with the Lord in prayer in order for our faith to produce results. Faith will help you overcome problems in your life and will keep you from being overwhelmed by them. When you have grown in grace, you no longer have to take your problems to God; you take God to your problems.

We must maintain a personal relationship with the Lord because our strength comes from our union with Him. The more time we spend in prayer, the stronger we become.

Grace is a divine influence upon one's heart and the reflection of the influence showing up in one's life in a heart that picks up on the impulses, inspirations, and ideas that come from the spirit of God. A heart that is attentive to the spirit of God picks up quickly on what the spirit is saying.

Grace gives you the ability to change the way you think about things and to line your thoughts up with how God thinks.

"'For my thoughts are not your thoughts, nor are your ways my ways,' says the Lord. 'For as the heavens are higher than the earth, so are my ways higher than your ways and my thoughts than your thoughts'" (Isaiah 55:8–9 NKJV).

God's thoughts are higher than our thoughts; therefore one must discern the thoughts of God. The things of the spirit must be spiritually discerned. One must be able to acknowledge one's own inability and one's dependence upon God. God's grace is working in our lives daily. It's God's grace working in you every time you make a change in your life.

Chapter 9 Questions

1. What is grace?
2. Grace gives you _____ over sin.
3. _____ grace is what saved you.
4. What does the Bible say all humans have in common?
5. Grace is a _____ from God.
6. What should every Christian be able to recognize?
7. _____ grace is God's ability working in you to stand in the ministry he has called you to.
8. _____ is about serving.
9. _____ grace is the ability to stand no matter what comes your way.
10. God's grace _____ you to overcome difficult situations without weakening.

Chapter 9 suggested Bible reading

Romans 23:10–12
Romans 5:19–21
Romans 5:1–2
Ephesians 2:8–10
Ephesians 4:7

Chapter 9 Answers

1. Grace is God's ability working in you.
2. Grace gives you power over sin.
3. Saving grace is what saved you.
4. The Bible says all have sinned and come short of the glory of God.
5. Grace is a gift from God.
6. Every Christian should be able to recognize what he cannot do under his own strength.
7. Serving grace is God's ability working in you to stand in the ministry God has called you to.
8. Life is about serving.
9. Standing grace is the ability to stand no matter what comes your way.
10. God's grace empowers you to overcome difficult situations without weakening.

Chapter 10

Prayer: What it is; and what it's not

Did you know that a great majority of Christians don't know how to pray? Many depend on the pastor or someone else to pray for them. Our relationship with the Lord is personal and our prayer life should be personal communion with God on a one-to-one basis.

Some religions teach prayer out of a prayer book, which makes prayer impersonal instead of producing a personal relationship with the Lord.

Prayer is not a formula. In the early 1980s someone came up with praying an hour, using the Lord's Prayer as a guide. For many it became a formula, a religious practice with no real power because they were lacking a personal relationship with the Lord. Many thought if they could pray one hour a day, it would bring them closer to God and He would be pleased with them. There are many things involved in pleasing God—not just prayer. Yes, prayer can bring one closer to God if he is praying according to God's Word, if he knows what belongs to him, and he understands what pleases God.

Prayer is not a chore. Prayer is communication with one's heavenly Father. There are principles of prayer that will work every time, if we do what the Word says. The Bible never tells us to come to God begging Him to do something. We are not beggars, we are children of God, and because we are children, we have access to Him and to what He has already given us.

If we want God to hear our prayers, we must come to Him praying His Word because His Word is His will, and the Bible tells us that when we pray according to His Word, He hears us.

"Now this is the confidence that we have in Him that if we ask anything according to His will, He hears us. And if we know that He hears us, whatever we ask, we know that we have the petition that we have asked of Him" (1 John 5:14–15).

If we don't believe God hears us when we pray, we can't pray with confidence. God wants us to come boldly to the throne of grace, not with fear and trembling but with confidence that He hears and answers prayer if we pray according to His will.

The Bible teaches us to enter His gates with thanksgiving and into His courts with praise. Praise should be common to the believer because God is good and is constantly loading us with benefits. If salvation was all we ever got from God, it would still be enough for us to be grateful to Him for the rest of our life. Salvation rescued us from sin's power and saved us from damnation. We have so much to be thankful for. Praise is the strength of faith while we wait for the answer to our prayers.

Most Christians enter His gates with problems and worries and complaints. There was a Pharisee who thought he was doing God a favor by the way he lived. One day he went into the temple to pray. In the temple was a poor man, also praying. The Pharisee started by reminding God that he wasn't like other men. He fasted and tithed and gave alms; he didn't steal or commit adultery as other men did. The Bible says he prayed with himself. God was not listening to his prayer. (L Luke 18:9-13) The poor man on the other hand recognized he was a sinner in need of God's mercy. You might be thinking I didn't know God was merciful to sinners or that He hears their prayers. He heard yours and He heard mine and had mercy on us. The Bible says this man went home justified. He was humble and recognized his need for God, whereas the other man was full of pride over his own accomplishments.

What if we went to God saying, "Father, I thank you for saving me, for forgiving all my sins, for meeting all my needs because you have never left me or forsaken me. Thank You for the peace I have in knowing you. Thank you that you always cause me to triumph in every area of my life. Thank you for Jesus. Thank You for Your Word. You are such a good God. You created me because you love me. You are the almighty God, the all-powerful God, the God who is more than enough, and the one who supplies all of my needs according to your riches in glory by Christ Jesus. You are the God to whom nothing is impossible, and nothing is too hard for you."

Do you think God hears that kind of prayer? When you pray this way, not only do you magnify God, but He becomes bigger and more powerful to you, and it causes faith to rise in your heart. The Bible says His ears are open to the prayers of the righteous. You are righteous because God has made Jesus, who knew no sin, to be made sin for us that we might be made the righteousness of God in Him. It wasn't because of what you've done but because of what He's done.

Before we tell God our problems, He already knows them. He wants us to come to Him in faith believing what He has already said in His Word. When we come to Him with the Word, the Bible says, He hears us. It also says He looks after His Word to perform it. If we don't pray the Word, He has nothing to perform. God uses His Word to create.

"That the communion of your faith may become effectual by the acknowledging of every good thing which is in you in Christ" (Philemon 1:6).

When we pray the Word, we are acknowledging who God is and what He's done for us, and it causes our faith to grow and become effectual. It produces results.

What Not to Pray

The Bible tells us that when we pray, we are not to make vain repetitions as some religions teach. God is not going to hear us because we recite prayers written by some man. God wants us to pray from our hearts. He doesn't want for us to repeat the same thing over and over. When we praise God, we are not repeating vain words. God's Word is never vain repetition. Jesus said we shouldn't pray to be heard of men. Some people pray loudly to be heard by others. It's done with the wrong attitude. Jesus said that when we do that, we have our reward. If we pray to God in secret, He rewards us openly. That's not to say we can't ever pray out loud. God looks at the attitude of the heart.

The Bible says that hypocrites love to make their prayers long because they think it will bring them notice in other words, don't spend all your prayer time talking. Has it ever occurred to you that God might have something to say? Prayer is communication with God. Why do we think God has to put up with our problems and our complaining? How many of us know that not many of our friends would put up with constant complaining? God is concerned with our needs, but He also wants us to know He is ready to meet those needs even before we ask.

How Do I Approach God?

Another thing Jesus said about prayer is that we are supposed to pray to the Father in the name of Jesus. Jesus said, "No man comes to the Father but by Me." We must come the way the Lord said. We pray in the name of Jesus because it is the most powerful name in heaven, on earth, and under the earth. It is the name that causes everything in heaven, on earth, and under the earth to stand at attention. Everything must bow at the name of Jesus on earth, under the earth, and in heaven. The name of Jesus carries authority in all realms.

Communication means not only that we set apart time to be alone with the Lord, but that prayer should be a lifestyle. God is real, He is everywhere at all times, and we can pray to Him anywhere at any time. My husband and I communicate throughout the day; I don't set aside an hour for us to communicate and then walk away and do my own thing. Marriage without communication is a marriage on the rocks. If we don't communicate with God throughout the day, our relationship suffers. Communication with God doesn't mean we're on our knees 24/7. We can communicate by reading His word, by praising Him with song, and by acknowledging Him in everything we do. We worship God and communicate with Him by our lifestyle. It makes no difference where you are; you can talk to Him anywhere, any time.

The more time I spend with the Lord, the more I love Him and the more dependent I become on Him. I become more aware of His presence, and more aware of His peace that follows me throughout the day. When I sleep at night, I go to sleep in peace with no worries because I know He takes care of me and everything that concerns me. When we become dependent on God, we cease from doing our own thing and become more aware of Him in our life. We have to let go of being the boss, of handling things our way, and of saying whatever comes to mind, and allow God to have first place in our life. When we do that, we cease from struggling. When we surrender to Him, we find greater freedom.

God will never let you down. Even if no one else stands with you, you know you are not alone. You and God are a majority. In Him you have the victory because God is faithful. You can tell Him everything and He will listen. Not only will He listen, but He will give you solutions you can't find anywhere else. God never judges you or condemns you. He is always there for you.

When I first started walking this new walk, I got inspired hearing people who pray talk about their experiences with the Lord. They had an intimate relationship with the Lord that I wanted. I didn't know how to pray, so it was difficult at first. I thought I had to be on my knees speaking to the Lord, and I didn't know what to say. As I read the Word, I became more knowledgeable of what God wanted from me. In His Word, I found out who God is and how much He loves mankind. I found out what pleases Him and that God is everything the Word says He is. It was through studying His Word that I came to know Him. Once I understood, and knew who God was, I could communicate with Him just as I do with my husband or my family. I didn't need formulas, and I didn't need religion; I needed relationship.

Knowing I'm His child and that He loves me made all the difference in the world because not having my earthly father in my youth; I didn't know how to relate to God as my heavenly Father. My father passed when I was fourteen, a very vulnerable time in my life. When I was able to understand God's love for me, my trust grew to the place where I now know that when I'm feeling down, I can go to Him and find rest and strength in His arms. I know Him so well that in sad times I literally feel His arms around me, holding me, and I feel secure in His love.

Prayer helps us become more Christ-like, to take on His characteristics.

According to 1 John 3:2 when He shall appear, we shall be like Him.

"For whom he foreknew, He also predestined to be conformed to the image of His Son, that He might be the firstborn among many brethren. Moreover whom He predestined, these He also called; whom He called, these He also justified; and whom He justified, these He also glorified" (Romans 8:29–30 NKJV).

The Bible teaches that we have been translated out of the kingdom of darkness and into the kingdom of God and that we are being transformed by the renewing of our minds. We are being transformed; it's an ongoing process. We are being conformed into the image of Christ. That also indicates an ongoing process.

To conform means to bring into harmony, to have the same form as another, to be obedient or compliant or submissive. Folks should be able to look at us and know that we are Christians. Our actions have changed, our words have changed, and people no longer see the person we used to be. In the book of Acts we see where people noted that the disciples had been with Jesus. We become like those with whom we associate. The disciples had been with Jesus, they acted like Him, and I'm sure they even talked like Him. Before we came to Jesus, people had no problem figuring out who we were acting like. Our actions portrayed our rebellion, and our disobedience and our words gave us away.

God is working in us; we are being conformed into the image of His Son, and He will continue working in us until the return of Jesus. The Word is our teacher. In the Word we see our shortcomings and the areas that we need to change. The Word of God brings correction and instruction in righteousness. We begin to see change take place as we continue in the Word and the Word gets in us and we become doers of the Word. As we begin to apply the Word to our life, we begin to take on His characteristics.

What were some of the Lord's qualities? He was meek, and He was moved with compassion; He was obedient to the Father, He never spoke of Himself, and He never acted on His own. He waited on the Holy Spirit. He demonstrated an unconditional love to the weak, the hurting, the sick, and those who were bound. Meekness is not a weakness. Meekness is a strength very few people possess. The world sees a meek person as a weak person because he is slow to anger, gentle and kind, and endures injury with patience and without resentment. Jesus was not only meek but humble. Meekness and humility are strengths every Christian should possess. One of the meanings of meek is the ability to accept the dealings of God without disputing or resisting. Meekness has no need to struggle with the dealings of God; it doesn't fight against God but welcomes correction.

The apostle Paul says in 1 Timothy 6:11 that we are to follow after righteousness, godliness, faith, love, patience, and meekness, which are all qualities of God. We as children of God should be growing and increasing in these qualities. These qualities aren't found in us just because we are children of God. We have to clothe ourselves with these qualities, and take off the old nature and put on the new, which is created in righteousness in Christ.

To know these things, we must be taught the Word of God and be instructed through meekness and gentleness. People don't change because their faults are being exposed. People change because they want to please the Lord. The Bible says it's the goodness of God that leads men to repentance. We must make it a practice of developing the fruit of the spirit in our everyday lives. Jesus lived and walked in the spirit, so He never had trouble with His flesh. We have opposition when we begin to walk in the spirit because of the old nature that was dominant in us until we came to Jesus. The old nature is the nature of the flesh and because we still live in flesh bodies, the old nature still wants to dominate.

In Galatians 5 the apostle Paul was making a contrast between the works of the flesh and the fruit of the spirit. The fruit of the spirit is the fruit that every child of God is supposed to be developing in his or her life. Developing the fruit of the spirit is an ongoing process; no person is born again one day and is fully developed in the fruit of the spirit the next. The fruits of the spirit are the qualities of the Holy Spirit that we as children of God are supposed to walk in on a daily basis.

The first fruit of the spirit is love. Love is the principal fruit because all the other fruit springs forth from love. If we love one another, we are going to treat each person as we ourselves would like to be treated. Love does no wrong to his neighbor. Love always puts the other person first and believes the best about that person. God is love, He doesn't have love; love is what God is. If we're being conformed into the image of Christ, then we must do what the Bible says. The Bible tells us no man has greater love than this, than to lay down his life for his brothers. Jesus is the express image of God's love. He expressed the love of God fully when He died for our sins, when He forgave all of our iniquities and healed all of our diseases, and when He paid the penalty for the sins He never committed.

God is good and gentle and kind even to the ungodly. He sends rain to all because God loves all of His creation. He stretches forth His hand and satisfies the desires of every living creature.

Chapter 10 Questions

1. Prayer is not a _____ and prayer is not a _____.
2. Prayer is _____ with our heavenly Father.
3. When we pray, we must pray the _____ because God's Word is His will.
4. The Bible teaches us to enter His gates with _____ and His courts with _____.
5. Prayer is begging God to hear us and do something. True or false?
6. Before we tell God about our _____, He already knows them.
7. Jesus taught us that when we pray, we should not make _____ as the heathen do.
8. God's _____ is His will and God looks after His Word to perform it.
9. We pray to the _____ in the name of _____.
10. Communication with God means we're on our knees 24/7. True or false?
11. You and _____ are a majority.
12. Prayer helps us become more _____.

Chapter 10 suggested Bible reading

1 John 5:14–15
Psalm 100:4
Matthew 6:8
Matthew 6:5–7
John 16:23–24

Chapter 10 Answers

1. Prayer is not a formula and prayer is not a chore.
2. Prayer is communion with our Heavenly Father.
3. When we pray we must pray the word because God's Word is His will
4. The bible teaches us to enter His gates with thanksgiving and His courts with praise.
5. False
6. Before we tell God about our needs He already knows them.
7. Jesus taught us that when we pray we should not make vain repetitions as the heathen do.
8. God's Word is His will and God looks after His Word to perform it.
9. We pray to the Father in the name of Jesus.
10. False
11. You and God are a majority.
12. Prayer helps us become more Christ-like.

Chapter 11

The Heart of a Servant

The church of today is facing a growing crisis. We're living in days when the love of many has grown cold, and people have become self-centered. "What's in it for me? What do I get out of it? How is this going to benefit me?" What happened to the heart of a servant?

When I was born again, it was in the late 1970s, and things were much different from what we're seeing today. People were eager to serve. We were encouraged to get involved and do something. We didn't have any knowledge of the Word, but we believed we should get involved in church. We volunteered at everything that came up. We helped in children's church, we helped in vacation Bible school, we greeted people who came in, and we got involved in prayer, in seminars, in Bible studies, in cleaning bathrooms, and in everything else our hands could find to do. Today one practically has to beg Christians to get involved. There are no volunteers because those who do anything for the church expect to be paid for their services. It grieves my heart to see this happening in our churches, and I know it grieves the heart of God.

God wants people who have a servant's heart: everything they do is as unto the Lord, without expecting anything in return. When God is looking for someone to promote, who do you think He is going to promote first? Is He going to promote the pew warmer or the person cleaning bathrooms?

Jesus was a servant. He said He did not come to be served but to serve. We talked about how we are being conformed into the image of Christ; shouldn't servant hood be one of the areas of utmost importance to the Christian? People who serve are people who give. They give of themselves, their time, and their finances. How did Jesus serve? When He saw a need, He took care of it. He didn't wait for people to come to Him; He went to them. It didn't matter to Him if the person was a leader, a tax collector, a sinner, or a saint. He never asked for anything in return. It didn't bother Him to be inconvenienced by someone's need.

The Bible gives us the account of a man named Jairus in Mark 5. This man was a ruler of the synagogue and had a young daughter who was at the point of death. He came to Jesus and asked him to go with him to his house to pray and lay His hands upon his daughter that she might live. Jesus went with him, and many people followed. While they were on their way to Jairus's house, they were interrupted by a woman who had an issue with blood. She had had the problem for twelve years and had suffered many things from many physicians but grew worse instead of better. This woman had heard of Jesus. He was her only hope. It was against the law for her to be out in public with an issue of blood. She risked being stoned if she was found out. But she was determined to get her healing no matter the cost. She was weak and sickly, but it didn't stop her from pushing through the crowd to get to Jesus. "For she said, if I may touch the hem of His clothes, I shall be whole" (Mark 5:28). She came and touched His clothes, and virtue went out of Jesus and she was healed. Jesus knew virtue had gone out of Him and He said, "Who touched my clothes?" The disciples said to Him, "You see the multitude thronging you, and you say, 'Who touched me?'" The woman finally came to Jesus and confessed that it was she who had touched his clothes and was healed. She began telling Him about the twelve years she had suffered many things of different physicians and wasn't any better and how she had spent all that she had. Jesus didn't let this inconvenience stop Him from listening to her, although men had come from Jairus's house to tell him his daughter was dead. Jesus just turned to him and said, "Do not be afraid, only believe," and went with him to his house and raised his daughter from the dead.

Jesus was never inconvenienced by the needs of people; He was always ready to serve their every need. One day when He and His disciples got out of their boat, they were met by a man who had a legion of devils. Jesus didn't ignore the man and tell him to leave them alone, not to bother them. This man was demon possessed. He cut himself with stones, lived among the tombs, broke the chains people bound him with, and was a terrible sight, but it didn't stop Jesus from stopping to deliver the man and set him free.

There are many examples in the gospels of how Jesus served people. One day as He and His disciples were walking down the road, a blind man named Bartimaeus was begging by the wayside. When he heard that Jesus was passing by, he began to cry out for mercy. The disciples wanted him to be quiet, but he began to yell louder. Jesus didn't walk by and pretend not to see him. He stopped and had them bring the man to Him and healed him.

What about the leper who came to Jesus and asked if He could make him clean? Jesus didn't stop to consider that the man was a leper, scorned by society as unclean. He never considered the fact that leprosy is contagious. He reached out and touched him, and the leprosy left. How long had this leper been without a human touch? When we came to the Lord, we were sinners and unclean, but He didn't reject us. He accepted us just as we were. Jesus didn't distinguish between a king and a leper or a rich man and a beggar; we all have sinned and come short of the glory of God. He never separated himself from sinners. Sickness and disease didn't scare Him away.

Our churches today want the world to come to them, but Jesus told us to go into the entire world and preach the gospel to every creature. Don't make a difference between the rich and famous and the down-and-outer. Both are important to God. Many church members don't want certain kinds of people coming to their churches because they don't meet the status quo or they come from the wrong side of the tracks. A person who has a servant's heart loves everyone and is always ready to serve them.

"Let this mind be in you which was also in Christ Jesus, who being in the form of God, did not consider it robbery to be equal to God, but made Himself of no reputation, taking the form of a bondservant, and coming in the likeness of men, and being found in the appearance as a man, He humbled Himself and became obedient to the point of death, even the death of the cross" (Philippians 2:5–8 NKJV).

The Bible tells us Jesus made Himself of no reputation. He didn't think too highly of Himself even though He was the Son of God. He humbled Himself and became a servant, and because He did, God highly exalted Him and gave Him a name that is above every name.

Jesus is our example. He is the one we are being conformed into the image of. Is Jesus a good example for us to follow? A servant clothes himself in humility. He sees a need and meets it.

What does God look for when He's looking to promote someone? He looks for humility and faithfulness, for one who does whatever his hand finds to do and does it without grumbling and complaining. A faithful servant is faithful in the little things. The Word of God teaches that if we are faithful in the little things, God will make us faithful over much. It also teaches us to be faithful in that which belongs to another, and then He can give us the true riches because we have shown ourselves faithful in that which belongs to another. No job is too small or too big for a humble person.

Luke 19:12–24 speaks of the Lord going on a journey and giving talents to His servants. He told them to occupy themselves with business until he returned. Two took their talents and gained interest, and Jesus said these were good and faithful servants, but one took his talent and hid it, maybe because he thought, it's such a little bit. What can I do with it? Many Christians hide their talents because they don't think they are worth much. We never know what the Lord can take and increase when we put it to use for His kingdom. Many Christians have hidden talents that are yet to be discovered. We will never know how far those talents can go or how much they can produce until we put them to work.

God blesses the work of our hands. Many ministers I know started out cleaning bathrooms even when it seemed their efforts were going unnoticed. Nothing goes unnoticed by the Lord. God sees everything we do, and we have to remember that promotion in God's kingdom does not come by man, but from God. Even though nobody sees, God sees, and what He sees, He rewards. Don't you want God's approval rather than man's? Yes, it's nice when somebody notices what you do, but if nobody notices, be assured that God takes note of it.

When I think of the heart of a servant, the story of Joseph in (Genesis 37-39) comes to mind. Joseph was a young man who dreamed a dream and told it to his brothers and his parents. His brothers were jealous of him and wanted to kill him but decided instead to throw him into a pit. Later they saw a band of Ishmaelites coming and decided to sell him as a slave. The Bible says God was with Joseph. He became Potifer's servant. Potifer saw that God was with him and prospered him in everything he did, so Potifer made Joseph a ruler in his house and entrusted him with everything he had. God made a leader out of Joseph. God's favor was upon him. Potifer's wife became attracted to Joseph and wanted Joseph to sleep with her, but he refused. One day as he tried to escape from her clutches because he was faithful to his master, she hung on to his robe. Later she accused him of raping her, so Potifer had Joseph thrown into prison, but in prison he was made leader of all the prisoners. No matter what situation he'd find himself in, God gave him favor. Joseph was able to interpret a dream Pharoah had dreamed and became the second in command in all of Egypt. In time there was a famine in all the land and he was able to be instrumental in saving his family. God made Joseph to prosper because he was found faithful.

In the story of Joseph we see how God promotes those who are faithful. Because of Joseph, his family was preserved through the famine. You never know whose life you are touching by your faithfulness or by your service to the Lord. Don't you want to hear the Lord say, "Well done, thou good and faithful servant; enter into the joy of the Lord"? Everything we do with a right attitude is credited to our account in heaven.

One day you and I will stand before the Lord and He will ask, "What have you done with the talents I gave you?" What we do for the Lord never goes unnoticed.

We should be serving one another—not counting the cost, but in sincerity serving one another with a right attitude. We should be looking for ways to bless people. God blesses us to be a blessing. There are many ways we can be a blessing. We can give of our time, our money, and our service. We can see a need and meet it and never wait for somebody else to do something we can do ourselves.

The Bible tells us that a faithful man abounds in blessings. Everywhere a faithful man goes, he encounters blessings. A faithful person is faithful in the little he has and when he has much. He always keeps his word even when he is rash in promising before he thinks. He takes care of things as if they were his own.

A servant doesn't expect rewards from man. A servant looks to the Lord and knows God rewards faithfulness. God's recompense is greater than anything mere man can give.

Chapter 11 Questions

1. God is looking for people who have what kind of heart?
2. _____ is our example of a servant.
3. What happened when the woman with the issue of blood touched Jesus' garment?
4. Jesus said to Jairus, _____.
5. A servant expects something in return for his service. True or false?
6. A servant does things without _____ and _____.
7. Who does God look for when He's looking for someone to promote?
8. A servant does _____ finds to do and does it as unto the Lord.
9. God wants to _____ you so you can be a _____.
10. _____ was a good example of a man with a servant's heart.
11. What did Jesus say about what He came to do?

Chapter 11 Suggested Bible reading

Mark 5:25–34
Mark 5:36
Genesis 12:2
Genesis 39:1–4
Matthew 20:28

Chapter 11 Answers

1. Servant's heart
2. Jesus is our example of a servant.
3. She was healed.
4. Jesus said to Jairus be not afraid, only believe.
5. False
6. A servant does things without murmuring and complaining.
7. He looks for someone with a servant's heart.
8. Whatever his hand finds to do.
9. God wants to bless you so you can be a blessing.
10. Joseph was a good example of a man with a servant's heart.
11. Jesus said He came to serve, not to be served.

Chapter 12

What Is Worship?

What is worship and why do we worship God? Are we worshipping only when we sing, or is our worship a way of life? I believe Christians should live a lifestyle of praise unto God, where their conduct, their speech, and everything they do brings glory to Him.

We've discussed how we must change the way we used to conduct ourselves before coming to the Lord. One of the things we talked about was our lifestyle, or conduct. A lifestyle of worship unto God means we are careful about our witness to others. Do they see Christians, or do they see the same conduct they see in the world? Our worship should show up in the way we talk, the way we act, and the way we honor God in our everyday life.

"But the hour is coming, and now is, when the true worshippers will worship the Father in spirit and truth; for the Father is seeking such to worship Him. God is spirit, and those who worship Him must worship in spirit and truth" (John 4:23–24).

Why is God seeking true worshippers? We have many Christian singers who produce music that is played on radio and TV stations everywhere. We have what we call worship services in church, and Christian concerts are very popular. Why then is God still seeking true worshippers? Worship is more than music and more than singing. Worship must have a purpose.

A true worshipper entails more than music and singing. A true worshipper worships in the good times and in the bad times, when things are going well and when they aren't. A true worshipper lives a lifestyle of worship unto God. His heart is right with God, and he lives according to the Word. Who should be the object of our worship? We have what we call worship songs, but when we sing these songs, is God the object of worship? Is the song directed at Him? Does it exalt Him as God? Does it lift Him up? These are questions I ask myself because throughout the years that I've walked with the Lord, I've heard very few songs directed to the Lord in worship for who He is. Yes, there are many great songs, but if you notice, most of them are about what God does and not about who He is.

I see that form of music as praise music, and it has its place. We should sing about the greatness of our God and what He's done for us. But God also desires worship from the heart. Praise makes one joyful. The Bible says we should rejoice in the Lord and shout for joy and sing songs of praise because praise is comely to the believer. Praise is like an ornament adorning every believer because we serve a mighty God. The Bible says we should shout unto God with a voice of triumph. Triumph means you are an overcomer, and God has made it possible. Praise keeps us conscious of what God has done for us, whereas worship keeps us conscious of whom He is, of His presence.

In a worship service, praise helps folks forget about their problems and reminds them that our God is big enough to handle any problem. It prepares the heart to enter into worship. Worship recognizes who God is and comes from a heart that knows God and has a personal relationship with Him. Worship arises out of our spirit as we communicate with the Lord. God is a spirit, and they who worship Him must worship Him in spirit and in truth.

What is a true worshipper? A true worshipper is one who is not satisfied with salvation alone. A true worshipper seeks a deeper relationship with God, and wants to be where God is and where God is moving.

I have found in my own personal life that I sense a greater closeness to God when I'm worshipping Him. That is usually the time I receive revelation and understanding from His Word. I truly believe the Word where it says times of refreshing come from the presence of the Lord. I have discovered those times of refreshing during worship. The book of Revelation tells us that in heaven, thousands of angels are singing and worshipping God and falling prostrate before His presence. I can't even imagine how wonderful it will be to hear those angels sing in one accord, in unison, and lift up worship to Him who sits on the throne and unto the Lamb forever and ever. God has delivered us out of darkness; He has forgiven all of our iniquities and healed all of our diseases. We have such a great salvation, and for that reason we should live a lifestyle of worship unto God. I like to believe that as we worship God, the angels join in.

The Bible tells us that the angels rejoice over one sinner who repents. Revelation 7:9–12 speaks of a time when a great multitude that no man could count of all nations and people and tongues shall stand before the Lamb clothed in white robes with palms in their hands and cry with a loud voice, saying, "Salvation to our God who sits upon the throne and unto the Lamb." When they say these words, the angels that are standing before the throne fall upon their faces worshipping God and say, "Amen: Blessing and glory, and wisdom, and thanksgiving and honor are unto our God forever and ever."

I truly believe the angels were present at the cross when Jesus died, and fully understood the price He paid for the salvation of mankind. They saw what His death, burial, resurrection, and ascension accomplished. Everywhere we see angels worshipping in the Bible they fall prostrate before the throne of God, on their faces in reverence to Him. It's awesome that they recognize the greatness of our God many times more than we do.

Nothing brings down the glory of God like genuine worship, and nothing touches the heart of God more than a heart that loves and honors Him.

The reason I like the song "Amazing Grace" is that I once was lost and now I'm found; I was blind, but now I see, thanks be to God! I once was bound, but now those chains that held me captive are gone! I am forever grateful for what Jesus has done for me.

As a new believer, you love God with a newfound love and appreciate what He's done for you. You must keep that newfound love fresh at all times because the cares of this world will come in and take away your joy. Many times you will feel like you've been abandoned, and you have to remind yourself that God promised to be with you always. You're just not going to feel Him the way you did in the beginning, and you have to walk by faith and trust the Word.

The Bible says we are to bring the sacrifice of praise into the house of the Lord. Why is it called a sacrifice? Because your praise unto God is not based on what's going on around you. It's not based on circumstances. It is possible to praise God in the storms of life, to give glory to Him at all times.

Worship recognizes God for who He is. It's a form of communication between God and man in the spirit. God is a spirit, and worship should come forth out of our innermost being—our spirit reaching out to God, who is a spirit.

A true worshipper is not satisfied with being where God has been; they want to be where God is. A true worshipper is willing to pay the price to get as close to God as he or she can. They don't care what people say about them or what they think, because they are concentrating themselves on the Lord.

Luke 7:36–47 speaks of a time when Jesus was invited to the home of a Pharisee, one of the religious leaders of that day. A woman known as a sinner in that city came into the house where Jesus was. There are several things that could have stood in the way, but she didn't let anything stop her from accomplishing what she came to do. She wasn't an invited guest; she wasn't the type a religious leader would have anything to do with. As a matter of fact, she was the type of woman who could be stoned. You can imagine the whispers going on: "Who invited her? What is she doing here? She's not one of us. Who let this sinner in?" She ignored their stares and their whispers; she wasn't concerned about what they thought. She was on a mission, and she wasn't going to let anything get in the way. She had eyes only for Jesus.

She took a box of very expensive perfume, probably the most valuable thing she owned, and without saying anything or asking for anything, she began to weep unashamedly, not caring what anyone thought. She began to wash Jesus' feet with her tears and dry them with her hair, pouring the perfume on Him so that the aroma filled the house. The Pharisee began to think to himself, If this man Jesus was a prophet, He would know what kind of woman this is, touching Him. Jesus knew what Simon was thinking. He turned to Simon and asked, "Simon, do you see this woman?" You know Simon was thinking, how could I not see her? Jesus was asking, do you see her heart, or do you see only what's on the outside? Jesus said, "Since the time I came in, she hasn't stopped kissing my feet. You didn't give me a kiss. She has anointed my feet with oil. What did you do for me?"

Jesus made a very important statement. He said, "Her sins, which are many, are forgiven, for she loved much, but to who little is forgiven, the same loves little." Of course the Pharisees immediately began to murmur because Jesus said her sins were forgiven. The Pharisees believed only God could forgive sins, and they didn't believe Jesus was equal with God.

Aren't you glad that God looks on the heart and not on the outward appearance the way we do? I suppose that's why Jesus said we are not to judge, because we see only outward appearances. We can't see the heart of man like Jesus can. He is the only true judge, the only one who can judge with true judgment. Many times we are too quick to judge by what we see. Only God can see the heart of a person.

When we come into the presence of God, there is no need for words. God is too awesome for words. Many times while in the presence of God, all one can do is weep because of the love one feels. God is the only one who can satisfy the human heart.

This woman had sought satisfaction in human relationships gone wrong. In so doing, she made many mistakes and committed many sins. When she found Jesus, the emptiness inside of her was satisfied, and all she could do was weep. At last she had found what her heart was longing for.

Many times the mistakes made in life stem from that hunger inside that seeks fulfillment. We look for it in different things that never can take the place of God in our heart. It's not until we come to the Lord with a repentant heart that we can experience true fulfillment. The void in us is satisfied.

As we continue to grow in Christ, we begin to know Him more and more and to understand His Word. Once the Word of God is understood we are able to apply it to our life and watch God change us from glory to glory. The more we give ourselves to the study of God's Word, the more established and settled we become, just like a huge rock that remains fixed no matter what comes its way.

I can look back in my life and see where God has brought me from. I don't ever want to forget it, because when we become too confident in what God has done for us, we cease to seek Him any further and we stop growing. We must always remember our foundation and continue to build upon it until Jesus comes back to take us all away.

I hope this book has helped you recognize who you are in Christ, and helped you build a foundation that cannot be shaken no matter what comes your way.

Chapter 12 Questions

1. What is true worship?
2. Why does God have to seek worshippers who will worship Him in spirit and in truth?
3. The woman who anointed Jesus with the very costly perfume was a _____.
4. Jesus said your sins are _____.
5. Why did the Pharisee get upset because Jesus said her sins were forgiven?
6. _____ recognizes God for what He's done.
7. _____ recognizes God for who He is.
8. Sometimes we must bring a _____ of praise because we don't always feel like praising God in the hard times.
9. Music and singing is what worship is all about. True or false?
10. Studying God's Word helps one become _____ .
11. The _____ builds a strong _____ in your life.

Chapter 13 suggested Bible reading

John 4:23–24
John 9:31
Luke 7:37
Psalm 116:17

Chapter 12 Answers

1. True worship is a lifestyle of pleasing God.
2. Because true worshippers are hard to find.
3. The woman who anointed Jesus with the very costly perfume was a sinner.
4. Jesus said your sins are forgiven
5. The law says only God can forgive sins, and the Pharisee didn't believe Jesus was God.
6. Praise recognizes God for what he's done.
7. Worship recognizes God for whom He is.
8. Sometimes we must bring a sacrifice of praise because we don't always feel like praising God in the hard times.
9. False
10. Studying God's Word helps one become established.
11. The Word builds a strong foundation in your life.

Chapter 13

Saving the Best for Last

At this time I would like to introduce you to a friend who sticks closer than a brother. He has been my helper, my strength, my counselor, and the one who reveals all truth to me.

"If you [really] love me, you will keep (obey) my commands. And I will ask the Father, and He will give you another comforter (counselor, Helper, Intercessor, Advocate, strengthener, and Standby), that He may remain with you forever. The Spirit of Truth, whom the world cannot receive (welcome, take to its heart) because it does not see Him or know and recognize Him. But you know and recognize Him, for he lives with you [constantly] and will be in you (John 14:15–17 AB).

Jesus was preparing to leave, knowing He would soon be betrayed and turned over to the enemy. He knew the time had come to fulfill what He had come to do. The disciples were very sad because they had walked with Him for three and a half years and now He was talking about leaving, and they didn't understand why. They had seen firsthand the miracles He performed. They saw Him raise the dead, heal lepers, and give sight to the blind. They saw the wisdom of God in the way He handled the situation when the woman caught in adultery was brought to Him. They saw His compassion as he raised the widow's only son from the dead and how He set the demon possessed free, but now He was talking about leaving. That's when Jesus began talking to them about the Holy Spirit.

Jesus said He would ask the Father to give them another comforter, one who would abide with them forever, the Spirit of Truth. He told them the world could not receive Him because they couldn't see Him or know Him, but that it wasn't so with them. He would come and dwell with them and live in them. Jesus went on to tell them that He would not leave them comfortless but would come to them. He was speaking about coming to them in the person of the Holy Spirit, who would live in them and lead them into all truth.

That same Holy Spirit is available today to every believer. The only requirement to receiving the Holy Spirit is that you be born again. Jesus said if He did not go away, the Holy Spirit could not come. Did Jesus go away? The Bible tells us Jesus is seated at the right hand of the Father.

Let me share a little of my own experience after I was born again. I mentioned earlier that I was born again in a little country church. We were taught about salvation and rededication just about every Sunday, but I began to feel empty inside, like I was lacking something, although I didn't know what it was. I had received Jesus as my Savior, but I didn't have a personal relationship with Him as I do now. I knew there was a change in my life because now I didn't desire the things I did before. I knew Jesus had saved me, but there was still a longing inside of me for something more. I didn't know what it was that I was missing.

Somebody gave me a book to read about the Holy Ghost and fire. It began to stir my curiosity, and I began to dig through my Bible and see what it had to say about this Holy Spirit I was reading about. As I read, I became more and more convinced that the Holy Spirit was the missing ingredient in my Christian life.

I set out on a quest to find Him but didn't know what I had to do to receive Him, so every time an altar call was made, I was up there praying and begging God to fill me with His Spirit. But

I still went away empty, the way I came. That was back in the days when people were taught to tarry for the Holy Spirit. We were told that if we cried and begged enough, He would come and fill us. Let me tell you, tarrying is not required to receive the Holy Spirit. All one has to do is invite Him in just as one invited Jesus. I didn't know that. No one told me it was that simple.

I believe it was at least a year before I experienced the presence of the Holy Spirit in my life. We were attending a missionary meeting in Houston when the Holy Spirit began to move and all 12,000 people hit the floor praying. When I got down on my knees, something wonderful happened. I knew the Holy Spirit had come to live in me. When I went to bed, I was praying, and suddenly I felt something that I can only describe as liquid love poured all over me. For the first time, I was able to see into the spirit world and hear the Lord giving me direction on certain things He was speaking to me about.

My life was never the same after that. A whole new world was opened up to me. Suddenly I understood the Scripture like never before. I was able to hear the still, small voice inside of me, leading and guiding me. The Holy Spirit has been my best friend since that day and has never left me. I sense His presence with me every day.

My husband and I have made missionary trips to Guatemala, Costa Rica, and Nicaragua, and every time I go, I sense the presence of the Holy Spirit stronger than anywhere else I've been. It's like a dome over me, protecting me, and I know He goes where I go because it is written in His Word that He will never leave me or forsake me. I've seen Him perform miracles and healings. It's easy to minister in those countries because the people are so poor, they need a power greater than themselves. They are hardworking people, working to provide their evening meal each day, and yet they have time to go to church every time there are services. I was going to say "every time the doors open," but most of their temples don't have doors or ceilings because they can't afford them. I see how different those countries are in comparison to ours. We are so blessed here and so enriched with goods that we can't see our spiritual condition and our need for God.

Up until the time the Holy Spirit came to live in me, I had never called Jesus my Lord, but now suddenly He became my Lord and master. The Holy Spirit made Jesus real to me. Now I was able to understand the price Jesus paid to set humanity free. I understood how much He loved me, and the Scripture began to come alive. It's like the Lord was sharing His heart with me. His desires began to become my desires, and all I wanted to do was please Him. I can never do enough to show my appreciation for all He's done for me. I know works can never take the place of obedience, so I endeavor to please Him by living according to His Word, by being a doer of the Word and not a hearer only.

First Corinthians 2: 9 tells us that there are things that eye has not seen, and ear has not heard; neither has it entered into the heart of man the things that God has prepared for them that love Him. But it doesn't say we can't see them or hear them or understand them. It says the Holy Spirit searches the deep things of God and makes them known unto us. He is the one who hears from God and then reveals God's Word to us. Unless we begin to search the Scriptures for ourselves, we will never know what God has prepared for us. The Holy Spirit agrees with the Word of God, and it's God's Word that He reveals to us.

The Holy Spirit is the one who helps us put off the old life and put on the new. He's the one who teaches us to walk according to the Word, and He helps us overcome the things that hinder and set us back.

I was born again in the days when much emphasis was placed on the Holy Spirit's role in the believer's life. It seems like these days, not much credit is given to the Holy Spirit. He's not welcome in many churches or services; many Christian denominations don't even believe in Him. It's sad because without Him we are limited in our knowledge and understanding of the Word.

The Bible says the Holy Spirit will glorify Jesus or He will cause everything we do for the Lord to bring glory to Him. Don't you want to give glory to the Lord? Our lifestyle demonstrates how much we believe the Word and how much of it we are putting into practice in our life.

A life that glorifies God is a life that is led by the Holy Spirit. A person led by the Holy Spirit is one who makes necessary changes when prompted by the Holy Spirit. He is always conscious of the Holy Spirit living inside of him. When we're conscious of the Holy Spirit living in us, we are careful about not offending Him or grieving Him.

If you want to know the plan of God for your life, the Holy Spirit is the one who can reveal it to you. Many Christians live and die and never fulfill the plan God had for them. How much do you want to do the will of God? Everything you think is God is not God. Just because it seems right or sounds right doesn't necessarily mean it is God speaking to you or directing you. As you grow in your knowledge of the Holy Spirit and you allow Him to work in your life, you are going to be able to distinguish between your thoughts and God's thoughts.

The Holy Spirit is a person; He is the third person of the Trinity: God the Father, God the Son, and God the Holy Spirit. Jesus called Him a him by gender, meaning a person. Jesus said that when He comes, He will lead us into all truth; He will glorify Jesus, being a person, the Holy Spirit has a personality, He has feelings, and He can be grieved. The Bible tells us not to grieve the Holy Spirit.

When the Holy Spirit is working in us, we are being conformed into the image of Christ, making us more like Jesus. We are being changed from glory to glory one day at a time.

If we don't know the Holy Spirit, He can't teach us. We have to be open to Him. We were taught to be open, teachable, and subject to change, which simply means we need to be open for new revelation from the spirit of God, have a teachable spirit, and be ready to make changes when the Holy Spirit is dealing with us.

How do I know when the Holy Spirit is dealing with me?

You will know when the Holy Spirit is dealing with you because you will hear Him on the inside as a still, small voice that you know didn't come from you. You didn't think it, it wasn't your idea, and it came from your innermost being. When He speaks to you, conviction will come, understanding will come, and the wisdom to know what to do will come.

"The spirit of man is the lamp of the Lord, searching all the inner depths of his heart" (Proverbs 20:27 NKJV). "For you will light my lamp; The Lord will enlighten my darkness" (Psalm 18:28 NKJV).

The Holy Spirit is the one who enlightens you in your spirit and will illuminate your understanding. It's like walking into a dark room and turning on the light. While it is dark, you can't see clearly, but once the light goes on, you are able to see clearly. The things you don't understand suddenly become clear, and all doubts are erased.

Why is it that many Christians never change? They can go to church every time the doors open, and they can say they are Christian but a change is never seen in them. They never renew their minds to think the way God thinks. They still think like the world; they never put God's Word to work in their lives. The reason is that they've never known the Holy Spirit; therefore, He can't teach them. Jesus said He would teach us all things. We have to be open to the Holy Spirit and willing to change when prompted. When the Holy Spirit reveals something to you, it becomes a part of you, and you will never forget it. When God's Word is revealed to you and gets down in your spirit, it begins to change the outside. We used to sing a song that says something on the inside working on the outside; there is something working on the inside of you that is going to manifest on the outside.

Many Christians spend their lives trying to be good enough, trying to do things for God, but without the Holy Spirit, life will always be a struggle because we can never be good enough on our own to gain God's favor. Jesus knew how man would struggle without a helper, and that is why when He went back to the Father, He sent the Holy Spirit to us.

The Holy Spirit is the revealer of all truth. Jesus said, "If you continue in my Word, then you will be my disciples. You shall know the truth, and the truth shall make you free."

Many denominations use the Bible to preach out of, but they don't understand it. It never changes lives because they need the Holy Spirit to reveal truth, and they don't acknowledge Him as God. Many teach that He is just a presence, a spirit that has no real substance. Remember, Jesus said that when the Holy Spirit comes, He will show us all things and bring all things to our remembrance. The Holy Spirit is the one who opens up the Word of God and causes it to make sense.

Did you know that the Holy Spirit is the author of the Bible?

"And so we have the prophetic word confirmed, which you do well to heed as a light that shines in a dark place, until the day dawns and the morning star arises in your hearts; Knowing this first, that no prophecy of Scripture is of any private interpretation, for prophecy never came by the will of man, but holy men of God spoke as they were moved by the Holy Spirit" (2 Peter 1:19–21 NKJV).

God inspired holy men of God to speak, and it was written as Scripture to teach us God's Word. The Bible says all Scripture is given by inspiration of God (2 Timothy 3:16). God inspired men by the Holy Spirit to write the Word of God. God still uses men and women today to speak under the inspiration of the Holy Spirit words of life that cause change in people's lives.

We need the influence of the Holy Spirit in our life to guide us day by day. The Holy Spirit is a person, and He has feelings much like ours; He has a personality, He has feelings, He can be grieved, and He can be quenched. We can communicate with Him just as we communicate with the Father and Jesus.

How does the Holy Spirit manifest Himself?

The Holy Spirit not only manifests Himself in signs, miracles, and wonders but does so daily in our lives by bringing conviction when we do wrong, by leading us, by showing us things, and by revealing God's Word to us. We must be ever conscious of His presence in our lives.

A person who is filled with the Spirit demonstrates the character of God in his or her life. A Spirit-filled person is one who gives of himself, his time, and his money. He loves people. He is faithful in all things; he reads and studies the Word of God and lives by it. Spirit-filled people are more tolerant of others because they recognize that not all Christians are mature and not all Christians walk in the Word. They aren't critical of others because they see their faults, but instead try to help them overcome their weaknesses.

We should be producing the fruit of the Spirit in our lives. "The fruit of the Spirit is love, joy, peace, longsuffering, kindness, goodness, faithfulness, gentleness, self-control; against such there is no law" (Galatians 5:22–23 NKJV).

We have studied the Holy Spirit as God the Holy Spirit, and now we want to see what the Bible has to say about the fruit of the spirit. This is the fruit that should be manifest in every believer's life that has the Holy Spirit dwelling in them. The Holy Spirit is holy; He doesn't need to grow and increase in the fruit of the spirit. We are the ones who are required to produce the fruit of the spirit in our lives. If we say we are filled with the Spirit, people should be able to see the evidence in our life. That evidence is the fruit that we produce by the power of the Holy Spirit living in us. These are qualities that God wants us to have so that the world can see the difference and recognize that we walk with the Lord. The Bible tells us to come out from among them and be separate. There should be something that separates us from those who don't know the Lord.

"I say then walk in the Spirit and you shall not fulfill the lust of the flesh. For the flesh lusts against the Spirit, and the Spirit against the flesh; and these are contrary to one another, so that you do not do the things that you wish" (Galatians 5:16–17 NKJV).

Walk in the Spirit and you will not fulfill the lust of the flesh or the cravings of the flesh or the cravings of a person who doesn't know God. The desires of the flesh are opposed to the Holy Spirit, and the desires of the Holy Spirit are opposed to the desires of the flesh. There is a constant battle going on inside of us; our spirit wants to do what's right and our flesh wants to do what's contrary to God's Word.

There is always going to be that conflict between the two. Before we were born again, we were governed by the flesh, or the human nature without God. After we are born again, we find that the flesh still wants to rule, but if the Holy Spirit lives in us, He will always want to do the right thing. Galatians 5:19–21 lists the works of the flesh, and we all know what those are because we all had the nature of the flesh before we were born again. Many people grew up in Christian atmospheres and Christian homes and didn't experience the things others have experienced in the world. Praise God for that, but not everyone was privileged to have that kind of life. Many of us came out of the world into Christianity stained by the world and the flesh, so we have more trouble with the flesh than those who didn't experience its lust. God didn't create us to know the works of the flesh. Adam and Eve's disobedience has caused all humanity born since then to be born with human nature, separated from God. Even after Adam and Eve sinned, it took man over 900 years for the effect of sin to be manifest and for death to take its toll on man.

Once man's carnal nature tastes something, it can never be satisfied. It just wants more and more, even if it's killing him. God wanted to keep His creation free from the effects of sin, sickness, disease, pain, suffering, and death. Sin brought all these things with it. That is why there is a battle going on between the spirit and the flesh. We have to fight to stay well; we have to fight temptation and fight to stay away from sinful things and fight to walk in the Spirit because the flesh wants its way.

The nature of God we now have is against the works of the flesh, but there's one dilemma here: we live in fleshly bodies and in a sinful world where anything goes, so we have to fight to walk contrary to the world. We must learn how to walk in the Spirit by obeying the Word of God. The Spirit of God only wants what's good for us, what will profit us, and what will give us the abundant life.

Change doesn't come just because we are born again; change comes as we see ourselves in the Word of God and obey it. God's Word is a mirror. It shows us our imperfections, our faults, and our shortcomings, but it doesn't leave us without a solution. In the Word of God, we find the solution to every problem. It's as we see ourselves in the Word of God that we begin to change. You can't be held accountable for what you don't know, but if you know to do well and don't do it, it becomes sin, according to the Bible.

The more deeply we walk with God, the more we understand the Word, and as we gain understanding of God's Word, it begins to transform us into the image of God.

There are nine fruits of the spirit just as there are nine gifts of the Spirit. I believe love is the principal fruit of the spirit because the other eight gifts of the Spirit proceed from love. If we don't have love, we can't produce the fruit. God is love; He doesn't have love. The very essence of God is love, and the Bible tells us that the love of God has been shed abroad in our hearts by the Holy Ghost. The capacity for love is there, but like any seed, it must grow and mature.

According to 1 Corinthians 13:4–8, love endures long and is kind. Endurance is one thing many Christians lack. They endure for a while, but when the going gets tough, they are gone. We may be able to endure long, but what kind of attitude are we displaying while we are enduring? Are we taking it patiently or do we become angry and upset easily, murmuring and complaining all the while? Love is never envious and never boils over with jealousy.

The apostle Paul said he learned to be content in whatever state he was in. It didn't come naturally to him; he had to learn it. We must be content with what we have, with how God made us. I used to live in misery because I was always comparing myself with other women. I never measured up. I wasn't tall enough or pretty enough or smart enough. I had to learn to love myself, to love me, whom God made in His image. You don't have to compare yourself with anyone, because God made you just the way He wants you. You are unique. God gave each one of us a uniqueness that makes us who we are.

Love is not boastful or vainglorious; love isn't all about me, all about what I want. Love doesn't get upset when it doesn't get its way. Love never boasts about its accomplishments. It's not conceited or arrogant or inflated with pride. Love is not rude or mean. Out in the world we learned to be rude because survival sometimes depended on it. It's not that way in God's kingdom. In God's kingdom everything works opposite of the world system. God's kingdom works by the law of love. There is no law that can be against the law of love. Love is the fulfillment of all the commandments and the law. The Bible says love is not fretful or self-seeking or touchy. Understanding the God kind of love shows us how to walk in the Spirit. Chapter 13 of 1 Corinthians is about the God kind of love. Love never takes an account of a suffered wrong. Out there in the world, we wanted to get even when someone did us wrong. God says, "Vengeance is mine. I will repay." Love forgives easily.

You can read 1 Corinthians 13 and read all about love, which is explained more clearly in the Amplified Bible. In reading the definition of love according to the Bible, you can see why the other fruit of the spirit stems from love. Walking in love produces joy, peace, longsuffering, kindness, goodness, faithfulness, gentleness, and self-control.

"If we live in the Spirit, let us also walk in the Spirit" (Galatians 5:25).

Chapter 13 Questions

1. Jesus said He would send us another _____ that He should be with us forever.
2. The Holy Spirit is our _____.
3. The Holy Spirit is the one who searches the deep things of God and makes them known unto us. True or false?
4. Is the Holy Spirit God?
5. The Holy Spirit has come to help us _____ the Christian _____.
6. If the Holy Spirit lives in us, the world should be able to see _____ of the indwelling Spirit.
7. The Bible says if we walk in the _____,we will not fulfill the _____ of the flesh.
8. Why do we have trouble walking in the Spirit?
9. We should be producing the _____ of the Spirit in our lives.
10. _____ is the principal fruit of the spirit.
11. There is no law against the _____ of love because love is the _____ of the law.
12. How many fruits of the Spirit are there?

Chapter 13 Answers

1. Jesus said He would send another Comforter that He should be with us forever.
2. The Holy Spirit is our Helper
3. True
4. Yes, He is God the Holy Spirit
5. The Holy Spirit has come to help us live the Christian life.
6. If the Holy Spirit lives in us the world should be able to see evidence of the indwelling Spirit.
7. The Bible says if we walk in the Spirit we will not fulfill the lust of the flesh
8. We have trouble because the flesh lusts against the Spirit, and the Spirit lusts against the flesh.
9. We should be producing the fruit of the Spirit in our lives.
10. Love is the principal fruit of the Spirit.
11. There is no law against the law of love because love is the fulfillment of the law.
12. There are nine fruit of the Spirit.

Suggested Readings on the Holy Spirit

John 14:26
John 15:26
John 16:7–16
Luke 24:49
Acts 1:4–5
Acts 1:8
Acts 2:1–4
Acts 2:38–39
Acts 5:32

Acts 8:14–17
Acts 10:38
Acts 10:44–47
Acts 11:15–17
Acts 19:1–6